1000m 750m 500m 250m 0m

5 6 7 8 9

25.8km 16.5km 14.3km 31.9km 15.3km

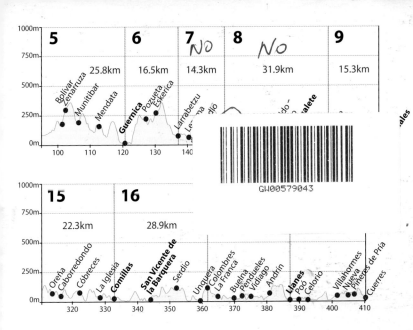

Bolívar
Zenarruza
Munitibar
Mendata
Guernica
Pozueta
Eskerica
Larrabetzu

100 110 120 130 140

1000m 750m 500m 250m 0m

15 16

22.3km 28.9km

Oreña
Caborredondo
Cóbreces
La Iglesia
Comillas
San Vicente de la Barquera
Serdio
Unquera
Colombres
La Franca
Buelna
Pendueles
Vidiago
Andrín
Llanes
Poó
Celorio
Villahormes
Nueva
Piñeres de Pría
Cuerres

320 330 340 350 360 370 380 390 400 410

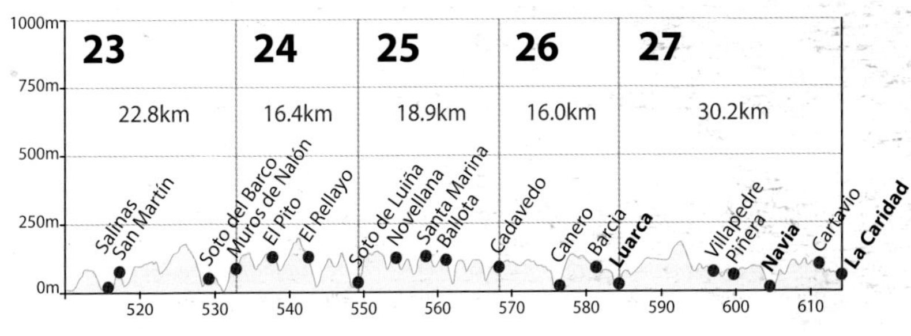

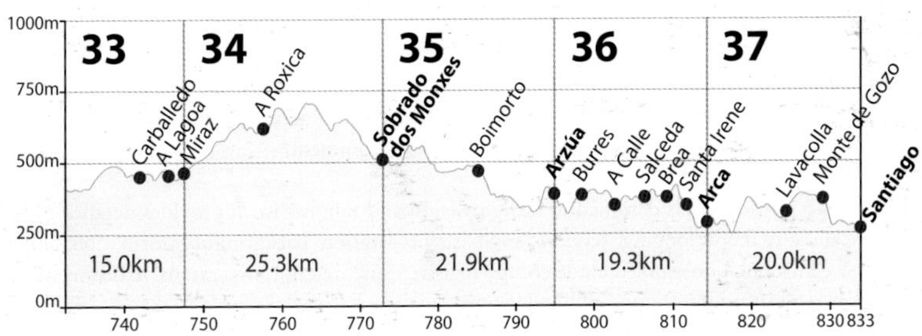

have more transportation connections, food, lodging and other services.

Camino del Norte: Irún to Santiago along Spain's Northern Coast
Matthew Harms, Anna Dintaman, David Landis
2nd edition, January 2019

Village to Village Press, LLC, Harrisonburg, VA, USA
www.villagetovillagepress.com

Photographs/Diagrams
All photographs and diagrams © Village to Village Press, LLC

Cover Photographs by David Landis
Front: Entering La Vega
Back (left to right): Leaving Llanes, Santiago Cathedral, Luarca

ISBN: 978-1-947474-10-9
Library of Congress Control Number: 2018902617

Cover and book design by David Landis

Disclaimer: *Every reasonable effort has been made to ensure that the information contained in this book is accurate. However, no guarantee is made regarding its accuracy or completeness. Reader assumes responsibility and liability for all actions in relation to using the provided information, including if actions result in injury, death, loss or damage of personal property or other complications.*

Note about town names: We generally use the Spanish name for cities and towns, though most also have a name or spelling in the local language (i.e. Guernica/Gernika). We occasionally use the local language name when it is the most prominent.

This **map guidebook** is designed to be lightweight and minimalist. It provides detailed stage and city maps, lodging, services, and basic preparation, background information, and tips. This book does not include comprehensive route descriptions, extensive historical background information, nor all hotel listings.

Visit **caminoguidebook.com** for more information.

Contents

The Camino del Norte

The Camino del Norte is a pilgrimage route across northern Spain beginning from Irún on the Spanish/French border and culminating at the cathedral in Santiago de Compostela, where St. James is believed to be buried. When people think of the "Camino" many are picturing the Francés route, traversing from St-Jean-Pied-de-Port over the Pyrenees into Spain to Santiago. In reality, there are many Caminos, echoing the ancient roads that pilgrims from Europe trod to visit the apostle's tomb. While the Francés route is most popular today, the Portugués and Norte routes come in second and third and continue to grow.

The Camino del Norte has rich historical significance as one of the oldest Caminos, reaching its zenith in the 9th and 10th century as the Muslim conquest of Spain was gaining ground northward, making the Francés too dangerous. The far north remained under Christian control, and the kingdom of Asturias, led by Alfonso II, remained one of the last bastions of control with its capital in Oviedo having its own famous relics of San Salvador. Pilgrims from all over Europe arrived by ship to the coast and made their way to Santiago without having to cross any major mountains. After the Reconquest of Spain in the 11th century, the Francés boomed in popularity as Oviedo's influence waned and the royal court shifted to León.

Today the route is reasonably well marked, and the number and quality of pilgrim services continues to increase. There remain towns and stages with inadequate albergue beds to match demand in the higher seasons, but pensiones and hotels have stepped in to offer pilgrim rates. Coastal sections of the trail pass through touristy beach towns where private lodging can be pricy and full in high tourism season (July/August); many youth hostels cater more to surfers than to pilgrims. Because the Norte has many fewer pilgrims, the route also has had fewer improvements and utilizes paved surfaces more than the Francés (around 69% of the route). The upside of fewer walkers means more solitude and less overcrowding.

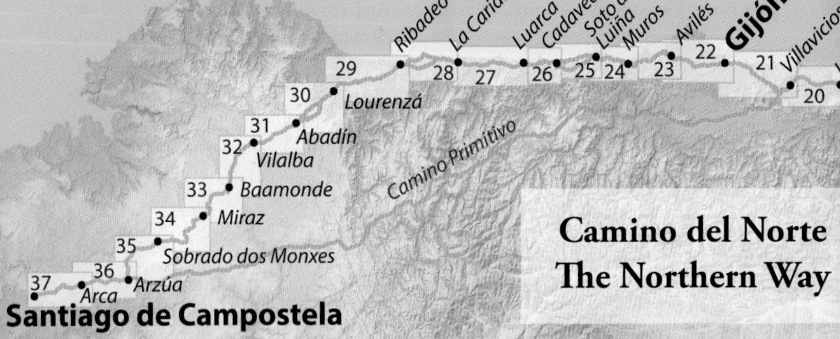

St. James

In the New Testament, St. James is referred to as a disciple of Jesus who left his trade as a fisherman to follow Jesus. The Bible tells us little about him, save that he requested to be seated at the right hand of Jesus in heaven and was present at many important events such as the Transfiguration and Jesus weeping in the Garden of Gethsemane. The last biblical mention of James is of his martyrdom by Herod Agrippa in 44CE. St. James became known as the patron saint of Spain not from biblical account, but from tradition, oral history, legend and myth. The story goes that James preached in Iberia with little success, attracting only seven followers. The Virgin Mary appeared to James with the pillar to which Jesus was tied to be whipped and instructed him to build a church in Zaragoza, Spain. Shortly after his encounter with Mary, James returned to Jerusalem and was martyred, and his body was transported to Spain on a stone ship without oars or sails, "carried by angels and the wind." The ship landed at Iria Flavia (present-day Padron), and James' disciples met the ship there and transferred his body to be buried on a nearby hill.

The body of St. James was forgotten until 813CE when a Christian hermit named Pelayo saw a light that led him to the grave. The bishop authenticated these relics, and King Alfonso II built a chapel to the saint. The event that catapulted this modest shrine to a major pilgrimage site was the mythical Battle of Clavijo in 852, when St. James was said to have appeared to assist the Christian army against Muslim invaders. This story mirrors Muslim legends about Muhammad appearing in battle to assist the Muslim forces, who were said to carry Muhammad's relics. This image of St. James was a convenient motif to draw Christian support to the frontier of Christian-Muslim battle and to bolster interest and financial investment in maintaining Christian domination of Iberia. The current cathedral was begun in the year 1075 and completed in the 1120s.

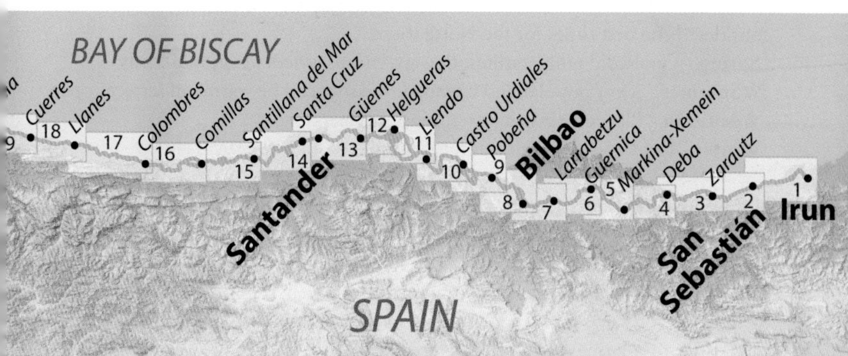

The Camino Experience

The Camino de Santiago is a network of historical pilgrimage routes throughout Europe that lead to Santiago de Compostela in Spain, the traditional burial place of Saint James. Rather than a remote wilderness trek, the Camino weaves through villages, towns, and even large cities. Walkers need not carry a heavy pack since frequent hostels and restaurants mean you can forego a tent, sleeping bag, and food resupply. The more popular Camino routes are well trodden enough that you can be practically guaranteed walking companions in any season other than winter.

Many undertake the Appalachian, Pacific Crest Trail, or similar for wilderness and solitude, neither of which are primary experiences on the Camino, which offers camaraderie, encounters with culture and history, and, for many, a spiritual experience. Since the Camino routes were used for religious pilgrimage, any walker is generally considered a pilgrim, even if walking more for sport than spirituality.

Pilgrim Practicalities

The ***Credencial*** or "**pilgrim passport**" is a document carried by Camino walkers that allows access to pilgrim lodging and also bestows free or reduced entry to some museums and cathedrals. Collect stamps (*sellos*) at accommodations and other landmarks, which serve as proof of completing the pilgrimage to receive a *Compostela*. The ***Compostela*** is a document of completion awarded to those who walk at least the last 100km to Santiago or complete the last 200km by bicycle or on horseback. Present your completed credencial at the pilgrim office in Santiago in order to get the Compostela, written in Latin and personalized with your name and date of completion. Be sure to collect at least two stamps per day for the last 100km. Cardboard tubes are available for carrying your Compostela back home.

When to Go & Trip Length

While the Camino can be walked in any season, summer and autumn are generally considered the best times for the Norte route.

Spring - Cool-cold temperatures, flowers, most services open, rain likely
☆**Summer** - Most popular and crowded, weather can be warm, all services open
☆**Autumn** - Pleasant temperatures, most services open
Winter - Cold and rainy with potential for snow, many services closed

How much time do I need? We recommend taking at least 6 weeks for the full itinerary to allow for a few rest days. We have divided the journey into 37 daily stages, with average daily distance of 22.5km (14mi). Feel free to deviate from this pace, staying at intermediary accommodations, which are noted on maps and in the text. If you have less time, consider starting in Santander (560km) or Gijón (350km), or walk one section such as Irún to Bilbao.

Visas and Entry

Spain is among the 26 Schengen states of the European Union (EU) that have no internal borders. Citizens of the USA, Canada, Australia, New Zealand, and some South American countries are issued a free visa upon arrival with valid passport, limited to 90 days within a 180-day period. Most African, Asian, Middle Eastern, and some South American nationalities must apply for an advance visa. Check EU regulations to see if your nationality requires an advance visa.

Sleeping

One of the unique features of the Camino routes is the network of affordable pilgrim lodging known as ***albergues.*** Albergues are simple **dormitory accommodations** intended for non-motorized pilgrims (traveling on foot, by bicycle or on horse). They are generally operated by the local municipality, parish, pilgrim confraternity, or a private owner. Many operate on a first-come first-serve basis, though most private albergues accept reservations. Lower cost albergues often fill up quite early in the day during popular seasons. On the Norte route, a number of cities open up a municipal building with bunks during July/Aug as makeshift albergues. In Galicia, public albergues are operated by the Xunta (governing body) and have a standardized price of €6. They tend to be basic, and kitchens often lack cookware.

Costs typically range between €5-15 per person, with a few on a donation basis (*donativo*). Amenities range from very basic to all the "bells and whistles" like wifi, washer, dryer, guest kitchen, etc. Amenities are shown in the text through symbols (legend on inside back cover). Accommodations with their own website have a symbol (links listed at **caminoguidebook.com**). Unless otherwise noted, assume that all albergues offer a mattress, pillow, bathroom with shower, and a place to handwash clothing. It's expected that you will bring a sleeping bag or sleep sack. The person in charge of an albergue is called a *hospitalero* (male) or *hospitalera* (female), and is often a volunteer. In areas with fewer dedicated pilgrim services, **hotels** and **pensions** often offer special pilgrim prices.

Spain offers a wide range of accommodations, from simple rooms with shared bathrooms in family-run pensions to opulent hotels. A **Hostel/Albergue** prices refer to a dormitory bed. If a hostel also has A H **private rooms**, the prices indicate dorm bed/single room/double room prices (€10/30/50). For H **hotels**, we list the single (if available)/double prices per room. Most albergues are open from around April 1 to November 1, with some staying open year round. Note that hotel prices are significantly higher in July/Aug. There are a few formal **campgrounds** on the route, but carrying a tent is uncommon as "wild camping" is not generally permitted, and reasonably priced lodging is available each night.

Eating

Cafes and restaurants are not as readily available as on the Francés route. We list town and villages with restaurants, but in smaller towns the open hours can vary. Larger towns and cities have grocery stores, and it is wise to carry some snacks. Dinner often consists of a *Menú Peregrino* with starter, main dish, wine, bread and dessert for around €8-12. Some lodging have a guest kitchen where you can cook your own meal. With special dietary considerations, such as gluten free, vegetarian or vegan, it may be challenging to find food that fits your needs in restaurants, especially since meat and animal products are staples of Spanish cuisine. Grocery stores in cities typically have a wide variety of foods including gluten free products, so plan ahead and carry some extra supplies.

Transportation

The closest airports to Irún are Biarritz (40min) and San Sebastián in Hondarribia (3km from Irún); Irún is also accessible by train. Common connecting cities are Madrid, Barcelona, London, and Paris. Other starting points with access include Bilbao, Santander, and Oviedo. Many of the cities on the Norte route are along the Renfe FEVE narrow gauge **railway line** as well as along ALSA **bus lines**. Local buses service many smaller towns, but with unpredictable schedules and infrequent service. The simplest way to skip a small section is by taxi. Hitchhikers are rarely picked up and should assume all known risks. Towns and cities with daily transport access are labeled with respective symbols in stage chapters.

Money, Costs and Budgeting

The unit of **currency** in Spain is the euro, made up of 100 euro cents. The best way to obtain euros is to use ATM/cash machines, available in cities and many towns marked in text with symbol. Pilgrim hostels and small town amenities work on a cash basis, but some hotels, restaurants, and shops accept credit cards. **Daily costs** for many pilgrims are simply lodging, food/drink and sometimes incidentals like first aid supplies, laundromat, or luggage transfer. An average daily budget probably falls in the €30-50 range, depending on your frugality, though it may be possible to spend a bit less and definitely to spend a lot more, particularly if you prefer hotels to hostels. Currency: US $1 ≈ EU €0.81, EU €1 ≈ US $1.23, EU €1 ≈ UK £0.88

Bed Bugs, a blood-sucking parasitic insect, are on the rise around the world and can be a minor problem along the Camino. While bed bugs do not carry any known diseases, bites can be very uncomfortable and cause painful rashes for some people, and they are very difficult to get rid of once infested. You can pretreat your sleeping bag and backpack with permethrin and check that any albergue you stay in has been fumigated recently to lower your chances of being bitten.

Phones and Internet

You can enable international roaming on your home mobile phone plan or purchase a Spanish SIM card (which requires an unlocked phone). International roaming on many US and Canada based plans can be quite expensive, but is a good solution if only used for emergencies. T-Mobile has free international data and text on some US plans. Calling and messaging apps like WhatsApp, Viber or Skype can be used when you have a wifi connection if you choose not to have cellular data coverage.

- To call Spain (+34) from the USA: 011 - 34 - XXX-XXXX
- To call the USA and Canada (+1) from abroad: 00 - 1 - XXX-XXX-XXXX

Wifi ("wee-fee") is increasingly available along the route; many accommodations and cafés offer free access. Some lodgings still have **desktop computers** for guest use while larger cities may have internet cafés.

Luggage Transfer

Transfer services cost **€4-5 per day**. Weight (<20kg) and distance (<25km/90km on bike) restrictions apply. The Post Office (Correos) provides luggage transfer from March 23-October 31. Book online, or call or WhatsApp +34683440022. Note that often public albergues don't accept walkers who use transfer services.

Medical Care

Spain has good medical care that is free for citizens and countries with reciprocal agreements. Citizens of Great Britain, Ireland and the EU need a European Health Insurance Certificate (EHIC). Non-EU citizens are recommended to have private health and travel insurance. Carry an emergency contact card with known allergies, pertinent medical history, and information that is helpful to medical staff if you are unable to communicate. In emergencies, dial 112 to reach emergency services. Pharmacies are well stocked and readily available in cities and larger towns.

Safety Issues

Spain has very low crime rates, and violent crime is extremely rare. It is always good to remain aware of your surroundings, not leave valuables unattended, and report any incidents to the police by dialing 112. Be extremely careful when walking along roads—always walk on the left side opposite traffic and remain alert. Try to avoid walking after dark. Aggressive **dogs** are not common but may be encountered. Carrying a walking stick can enhance confidence when encountering animals. All dogs in Spain are required to be vaccinated against rabies.

Additional planning information is available online at **caminoguidebook.com** and **caminocyclist.com**.

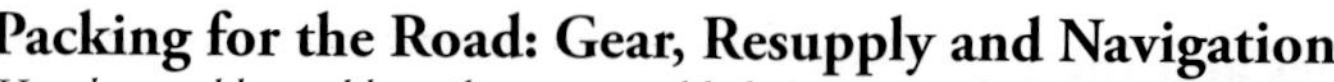

Packing for the Road: Gear, Resupply and Navigation

He who would travel happily must travel light. -Antoine de Saint-Exupéry

A light load makes for a happy pilgrim, and weight should be a primary concern in packing. A popular guideline is to pack no more than 10% of your body weight. Resist the temptation to pack many extras "just in case." Shops are readily available in Spain and most anything lacking can be purchased along the way.

Backpacks: A 30-40L (1800-2500in^3) pack is sufficient for warm weather (40-50L for winter). Measure your torso length and choose a pack of the proper size, preferably being fitted at a knowledgeable outdoor retail store. Aim for a pack that weighs less than 1.4kg (3lbs) when empty.

Footwear: Light boots or sturdy trail runners with a stiff or semi-rigid sole offer protection for your feet and ankles against the often hard-surfaced, rocky and uneven path (trail surfaces, p. 14). Get fitted for footwear in the afternoon or evening after feet have expanded during the day. Bring some kind of lightweight footwear to wear in the evenings, such as flip-flops or foam sandals. ⚠ Be sure to thoroughly break in your footwear before beginning the Camino with practice hikes wearing your loaded pack. Invest in wool socks (not cotton), which wick moisture away from your skin, dry quickly, insulate when wet and manage odor better. If you're prone to blisters, experiment with liner socks (wool or polypropylene) to create an extra rubbing layer other than your skin.

Sleeping Bags: Most pilgrims prefer a lightweight, mummy-style, 1-season summer sleeping bag (rated $^+$40+°F/$^+$5+°C) for the summer season. Some opt for only a sleeping bag liner in the heat of summer. For winter and the cool edges of fall and spring, it's a good idea to have a 3-season sleeping bag (rated $^+$15-$^+$35°F/$^-$10-0°C. Buy the lightest bag you can afford within your desired temperature range.

Clothing: Consider hiking clothes as layers, with inner layers for moisture management, middle for insulation, and outer for weather protection. The general rule for outdoor clothing is to avoid cotton as it does not retain insulating properties when wet and dries slowly. Synthetic materials (polyester, nylon, spandex) and wool (especially merino) are preferred, especially in cold and wet weather. In warm seasons, choose lightweight breathable clothes that provide sun protection.

Be prepared for the sun with a wide-brimmed **hat** and **sunglasses,** and use **sunscreen** regularly. Bring a **lightweight rain jacket** with a waterproof breathable membrane, or use a poncho that can also cover your backpack. Bring a waterproof pack cover or line your pack with plastic garbage bags to keep your gear dry. Pack electronics in zippered plastic bags or dry bags to protect against moisture.

Hypothermia is possible in wet, cool weather (as is common on the Norte route), so be prepared with a dry set of clothes (socks included) for after a rainy day, and bring one insulating layer, such as a warm fleece or down sweater.

Water and refills: While water is readily available most days of the Camino, it is important to carry sufficient amounts. Always carry at least one liter, and refill often. Carry more than two liters on hot days or in more remote areas. Reliable water refill sites are marked on stage maps (🚰). Tap water in Spain is treated and drinkable (*potable*). Most historic springs are marked as undrinkable (*no potable*) because they have not been treated or tested. Bottled water is widely available, but less environmentally-friendly than refillable bottles.

Dehydration and heat-related illness: Dehydration can lead to fatigue, headaches, heat exhaustion, and heat stroke (a dangerous and life-threatening condition). Be sure to eat foods that help to replenish electrolytes and consider an electrolyte drink, such as Aquarius™, on hot days. If you become dehydrated and overheated and are unable to cool down, take a break in a cool, shady place, rehydrate with electrolytes and cool with a wet cloth or fanning until you feel better.

Fitness and Training: The Camino is not a technically challenging hike, but the journey's length and hard surfaces day after day takes a toll on the body. Taking the time to practice before beginning the pilgrimage will greatly reduce possible injuries. Training walks will help you get used to your gear, the weight on your feet and shoulders, and any other potential issues you might be able to prevent. It's wise to get used to full-day walks, taking 2-3 shorter walks per week and one full-day walk weekly with your loaded backpack. Check with your doctor if you have concerns about your health or fitness level, and start out slow and gradual.

Blister Prevention: The most common injury can cause an end to your trip.

- At home: choose properly fitting footwear. Try on many options before buying (foot should not move or slip when walking on various terrain types and grades). Use wool socks and liners. Break in footwear by taking hikes with a loaded pack prior to beginning the Camino.
- On the trail: keep feet cool and dry, take off shoes and socks for breaks, wash feet and socks daily, use liner socks.

Packing List

Hiking Gear Essentials

- ☐ **Backpack** (30-40L)
- ☐ **Sleeping bag or bag liner**, lightweight
- ☐ **Navigation**: guidebook, GPS (optional)
- ☐ **Headlamp** or flashlight/torch
- ☐ **Sun protection**: hat, sunglasses, sunscreen and lip balm
- ☐ **Towel**, lightweight travel type
- ☐ **Water bottles** and/or **hydration system** (2L)
- ☐ **Waterproof pack cover/poncho**
- ☐ **Pocket/utility knife** (checked luggage)
- ☐ **Lighter** or **matches** (buy locally)
- ☐ **Toiletries** (list opposite)
- ☐ **Personal items** (list opposite)
- ☐ **First aid kit** (list opposite)

Take the time to visit a quality outdoor gear shop to get fitted for a backpack that is comfortable and footwear that fits properly.

Footwear & Clothing

- ☐ **Footwear** (boots or trail runners)
- ☐ **Sandals** or flip-flops
- ☐ **Hiking socks** (3 pairs wool)
- ☐ **Sock liners** (1-2 pairs wicking)
- ☐ **Pants** (1-2 pairs quick-drying, zip-offs, or shorts)
- ☐ **Short-sleeved shirts**, tank tops (1-2)
- ☐ **Long-sleeved shirts** (1-2)
- ☐ **Light fleece** or jacket
- ☐ **Waterproof jacket** or poncho
- ☐ **Underwear** (3 pairs)
- ☐ **Sports bras** (2)
- ☐ **Bandana** or Buff
- ☐ **Swimsuit** (optional)
- ☐ **Warm hat***
- ☐ **Insulating jacket***
- ☐ **Long underwear** top/bottom*

**only necessary in cold seasons*

Additional Gear (Optional)

- ☐ **Hiking poles**: Used correctly, poles can take up to 25% pressure off of your leg joints. Poles are great for stability, especially going up and down hills, and serve double-duty as a means to chase away dogs. Worthwhile for anyone with joint issues. Inexpensive poles can be purchased in on route.
- ☐ **Sleeping mat**: A lightweight foam pad can come in handy for sitting on and for sleeping if albergues are full or have limited beds. You can often find left behind mats for free along the Camino.
- ☐ **Pillowcase**: Most albergues have pillows but do not change the pillowcases regularly, a spare T-shirt can also be stretched over the pillow as a makeshift case.
- ☐ **Stuff sacks** or cloth bags with drawstrings don't weigh much and keep you organized
- ☐ **Reusable nylon grocery bag**: Comes in handy as a laundry bag, purse and grocery bag
- ☐ **Clothespins** or safety pins for hanging laundry.
- ☐ **Travel cooking pot and utensils**: Many of the albergues in Galicia have kitchens, but no kitchen equipment whatsoever. If you are intent on cooking your own dinners, you may wish to bring a lightweight cooking pot, or purchase one when you arrive in Galicia.
- ☐ **Camping gear:** Lightweight tent (TarpTent) or bivy sack, camping stove, a pot and utensils, and extra water carrying capacity. (See Camping p. 7).

***For recommendations on specific brands and models, visit caminoguidebook.com.**

***Decathlon** is a chain of outdoor gear retailers throughout Spain with stores in Irún, Bilbao, Santander, Gijón, Oviedo, and Santiago de Compostela, as well as Madrid and Barcelona.

Toiletries

Don't pack too much. Bring small refillable travel bottles of shampoo and conditioner <100mL/4oz. Refill from items left behind (ask at the albergues) or buy your own refill and share.

- ☐ **Shampoo/conditioner** (100mL/4oz bottles)
- ☐ **Toothbrush** and **toothpaste** (travel sized)
- ☐ **Soap**, biodegradable bar or liquid, such as Dr. Bronner's™
- ☐ **Laundry detergent** (powder works well and weighs less) or 100mL/4 oz. bottle or solid bar
- ☐ **Toilet paper** or tissues (albergues frequently run out)
- ☐ **Deodorant** (optional, you will stink with or without it!)
- ☐ **Hand sanitizer** (optional)
- ☐ **Contact solution** (if necessary), replace at pharmacies

First Aid/Medical Kit

Supplies are available in pharmacies along the route and most albergues have a basic medical kit. It's always best to be prepared with at least a few day's worth of each supply. Keep it light!

- ☐ Any **prescription medicine** you need
- ☐ Variety of **Band-Aids®/plasters, sterile gauze pads**
- ☐ Antiseptic towelettes or **wound disinfectant**
- ☐ **Antibiotic ointment**
- ☐ **Medical tape**
- ☐ **Elastic bandage** (such as ACE™)
- ☐ **Pain reliever/fever reducer** (such as acetaminophen or ibuprofen)
- ☐ **Antihistamine** (such as Benadryl®)
- ☐ **Anti-diarrheal** medicine: loperamide hydrochloride (Imodium®)
- ☐ **Blister treatment** (such as Moleskin or Compeed®)
- ☐ **Safety pins**
- ☐ **Baby powder** (helps with chafing)
- ☐ Small **scissors** and **tweezers**

Personal Items (Optional)

- ☐ **Travel wallet**: with passport/ID, health insurance card, pilgrim passport, money, credit cards, ATM card, etc. Stash an extra ATM card or wad of cash somewhere separate from your wallet.
- ☐ **Earplugs**: high quality noise-canceling earplugs are essential for a good night's sleep.
- ☐ **Mobile phone** and **charger** (see Phones and Internet p. 9)
- ☐ **Camera, charger, memory cards**, compact USB flash drive for backup
- ☐ **Journal with pen/pencil**: highly recommended for remembering the details of each day, reflecting more fully on the experience and recording contact info of new friends.
- ☐ **Tablet or e-reader:** useful for checking email and for pleasure reading without carrying heavy books. Photos of family and home are good conversation starters.
- ☐ **Book** for pleasure reading (just bring one and trade when you're done)
- ☐ **Plug/currency converter** for any electrical appliances (European plugs run on 220V with two round prongs. Most electronics run on 110-220V, labeled on device, requiring only a plug converter and not a currency converter.)
- ☐ **Zippered plastic bags or waterproof stuff sacks** for keeping electronics and other valuables dry and organized.
- ☐ **Pilgrim's shell**

Blister Treatment

- Take a break, remove socks to let feet cool and dry out. Check for hot spots and address by applying moleskin, Compeed®, or duct tape to create an additional rubbing surface to protect the hot spot.
- If a blister forms, use a sterilized needle to puncture its edge near the skin and drain using sterile materials. Air dry and re-dress blister with sterile bandages.
- If the blister or surrounding area becomes infected over the course of several days (increasing red appearance, tenderness, pus, red streaks), seek medical attention.

For **dry and cracked feet**, consider wearing socks all the time to keep moisture in for cracks to heal. In severely painful cracks, a tiny bit of super glue can be helpful to hold the crack together, but make sure to clean the area thoroughly with soap, water, and antiseptic.

Impact-related injuries are common with the large amount of paved surfaces on the Camino. If your feet and joints are taking a pounding, consider reducing your daily distance, walking on the softer shoulder near the paved path, or adding walking poles and/or thicker socks.

The Trail: The paths that make up the Camino de Santiago covered in this book span over 800km (500 miles) and vary greatly in trail surface, grade, landscapes, ecosystem, and climate. Proportionately, the Camino has more paved surfaces than many hikers expect, including sections of cobblestone, contributing to stress on feet and joints. P Paved / U Unpaved designations in this book refer to most obvious walking surface. There may be unpaved shoulders or footpaths along paved roads.

Route Finding, Trail Markings, Maps and GPS ➡ The Camino del Norte is generally well marked, with a few sections where marks are more scarce and faded. The most common waymarks are painted yellow arrows ➡, though a variety of other markings exist in different regions that incorporate yellow arrows or scallops shells into posts or signs. The most difficult sections to navigate are through large cities, where routes are often poorly marked and Camino markers compete with other signs. For this reason,

The path is well marked with yellow arrows.

we've included a number of detailed city maps throughout this book, though note that the maps are representative and not exhaustive, without every street name. When there is more than one marked route option, we provide a brief overview of both options and show them numbered on the map. **GPS route files are on our website, as well as tips on smart phone navigation.**

Daily Stages and Regional Sections: This book organizes the Camino del Norte into 37 daily stages averaging about 22.5km (14 miles) per day. The page spreads introducing each stage include a stage map, elevation profile, total distance, paved/unpaved (P/U) percentages, difficulty level (see below), time estimate, and a list of towns with albergues/pilgrim lodging.

Stages begin and end at the main or largest albergue in the beginning and ending locality whenever possible. For mid-stage towns and points of interest without albergues, measurements are taken from the town center or main church, whichever is prominent or closest to the marked route. Cumulative stage distances are noted on the stage maps and correspond to distances listed in town listings and elevation charts. Distances for off-route accommodations or points of interest are indicated with a plus symbol (example: +1.3km). Towns list resources available, all the albergues, and a selection of private accommodations in varying price ranges.

Distances are measured in kilometers and meters. Estimated **walking time** for each stage assumes a pace of 3-4 km/hr (1.8-2.5 mph) with difficulty in terrain and elevation change considered. Factor extra time for breaks and exploration. Each day's stage route is assigned a **difficulty level** from 1-3. These ratings consider an "average" walker, who is reasonably fit but not necessarily athletic.

Length:
1m = 1yd or 3ft
100m ≈ 100yd
1km = 0.62 miles
10km = 6.2 miles
1.6km = 1 mile

Easy: Slight elevation change, sturdy footing, water easily accessible
Moderate: Some elevation change, moderately challenging terrain
Challenging: Significant elevation change, possibly rocky or narrow path with less stable footing, water and other amenities may be scarce

This **map guidebook** is designed to be lightweight and minimalist. It provides detailed stage and city maps, pilgrim lodging as well as select hotels, listing of amenities in relevant towns and cities, and basic preparation, background information, and tips when helpful. This book does not include comprehensive route descriptions, extensive historical background information, nor all hotel listings.

Visit **caminoguidebook.com** for expanded planning information.

1

IRÚN TO SAN SEBASTIÁN

26.1km (16.2mi), **8-10.5 Hours, Difficulty:**

P 48%, 12.5km, U 52%, 13.6km

Irún is often considered the starting point of the Camino del Norte, though some pilgrims start further east in France. Our map starts from the bridge spanning the Bidasoa River that connects Irún to French Hendaye, but many pilgrims start ~2km closer, near Irún's central train station, where markings are better maintained. From Irún, you'll immediately experience some of the Camino del Norte's more significant climbs. Unsurprisingly, the day's climbs offer many spectacular vistas—some of the most stunning of the entire route!

Shortly after the Santuario de Guadalupe (an ideal rest stop with wonderful views of the Bay of Biscay and French coast past Hondarribia), there are ⚠ **two route options.** ❶ The route highlighted on the map follows a dirt road along a forested mountainside with sporadic views of the Basque interior. ❷ The second option (highly recommended if you can manage the initial climb), ascends very steeply along a footpath, climbing 100m of elevation over 300m, before continuing more gradually along a ridgeline to a high point at 545m. The many spectacular views in all directions make the initial climb well worth the effort. The high route is 1km shorter than the low route. Where these routes rejoin on a dirt road heading west (slightly uphill), another marked route goes southwest (downhill) to Lezo—best to just follow the dirt road here. For a shorter day, consider staying in Pasajes de San Juan; the albergue overlooks the Pasaia River.

0.0 **Irún** A H

1. **A Jakobi** (muni, 60, don): , Lesaka 1, 640361640, 4pm Mar-Oct, new location as of 2018
2. **H Bidasoa** (€40/50): , Estación 14, 943619913, mixed reports
3. **H Gema** (€30/40): , Estación 5, 661172552
4. **H Lizaso** (€35/45): Aduana 5, 943611600
5. **H Bowling** (€40/50): , Mourlane Michelena 2, 43611452
6. **H Alcazar** (€68/75): W D, Iparralde 11, 943620490
7. **H Pensión Europa** (€41-59/57-84): W D, Iparralde 59, 943622144
8. **H Aitana** (€55-81/67-102): W D, Iparralde Hiribidea, 943635700

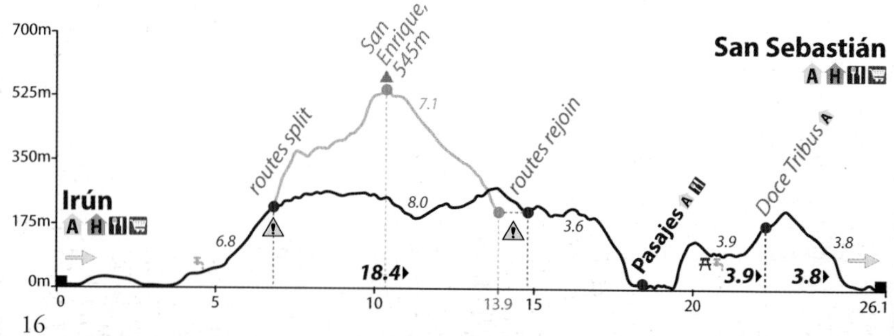

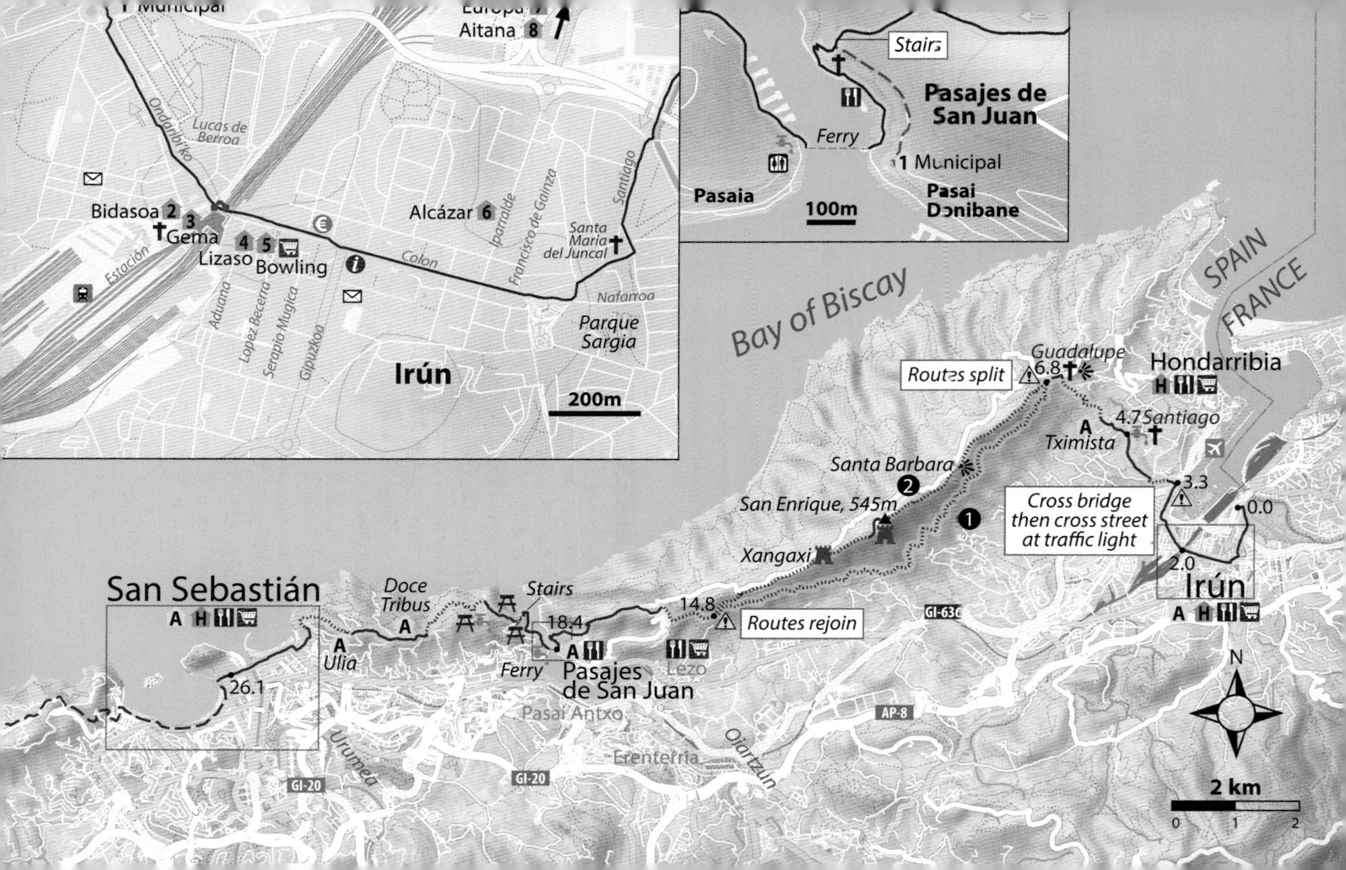
Aitana 8
Bidasoa 2
3
Gema
Lizaso
4 5
Bowling
Alcázar 6
Ondaribi'ko
Lucas de Berroa
Estación
Aduana
Lopez Becerra
Serapio Mugica
Gipuzkoa
Colon
Iparralde
Francisco de Gainza
Santiago
Santa Maria del Juncal
Nafarroa
Parque Sargia
Irún
200m
Stairs
Pasajes de San Juan
Ferry
1 Municipal
Pasaia
Pasai Donibane
100m
Bay of Biscay
SPAIN
FRANCE
Hondarribia
Guadalupe
6.8
Routes split
4.7 Santiago
Tximista
Santa Barbara
3.3
0.0
2.0
Cross bridge then cross street at traffic light
San Enrique, 545m
Xangaxi
Irún
San Sebastián
Doce Tribus
Stairs
14.8
18.4
Routes rejoin
GI-636
Ulia
Ferry
Pasajes de San Juan
Lezo
26.1
Pasai Antxo
AP-8
Urumea
Erenterria
Oiartzun
GI-20
GI-20
N
2 km
0
1
2

4.7 **Hondarribia** A H Map on page 17.

The San Sebastián Airport is in Hondarribia, north of Irún. From Hondarribia, a marked route leaves the city center and joins the Camino route from Irún at La Ermita de Santiago.

A **Capitán Tximista** (40, €20-22): , Jaizubia 14, 943643884, all year, just off route 3.3km past Irún Train Station

H **Maidanea** (€56/70): Lugar Barrio Arkoll 48, 943640855, 2km past Irún station

H **Arrobígaín** (€55): , Arkolla Auzoa 60, 672326626, 2.8km past Irún station

H **Arrotzenea** (€55-77): , Barrio Arkoll, 943642319

H **Obispo** (€100+): , Apezpiku Kalea 1, 943645400

H **Higeralde** (€62+): , Higer Bidea 6, 679847727

H **Villa Magalean** (€160-450): , Nafarroa-Behera Kalea 2, 943569130

H **Parador** (€180+): , Plaza de Armas 14, 943645500

H **Palacete** (€70+): , Gipuzkoa Plaza 5, 943640813

18.4 **Pasajes de San Juan** A , Basque: *Pasai Donibane.* Before the final flight of stairs to the water's edge, a path turns south to the A (map p. 17).

A **Santa Ana** (muni, 14, don): , Donibane 1, 943340177 4pm April - Oct 15

A ferry connects Pasai Donibane to Pasaia, which runs every few minutes during the day (Mon-Thurs: 6:30am-11:00pm; Fri: 6:30am-12:00am; Sun/Holidays: 7:45am-11:00pm). The ride across costs €0.70. On the other side of the river, after walking along the river toward the coast, you have a steep climb out of town up a stairway, but at the top of the climb the grade evens out.

26.1 **San Sebastián** A H , Basque: *Donostia.*

This touristic city has many private youth hostels and lodging options. The municipality opens the Claret Ikastola school (1.2km before city center) for pilgrim lodging July/Aug and operates La Sirena youth hostel (3km past city center) year-round that also caters to pilgrims.

1. A **Claret Ikastola** (60, don): Navarra 1, 943427281, 3pm, July/Aug only
2. A **La Sirena** (102, €15-25): , Igeldo 25, 943310268, , near beach
3. A **Downtown River** (€20+): , San Martín 2, 943563466, central
4. A H **A Room in the City** (€20+/-/50+): , Easo Kalea 20, 43429589
5. A **Doce Tribus** (par, 15, don): , Paseo de Ulía 375, 943327983, all year, 3.8km before San Sebastián, dorm separated by gender
6. A H **Ulía Youth Hostel** (62, €15-20/-/46+): , Ulia Pasealekua 297, 943483480, all year, 2.5km before San Sebastián
7. H **Casa Nicolosa** (€59+): Aldamar 4, 943430143
8. H **Hospedaje Kati** (€20-25/person) , Fermín Calbetón 23, 943430487
9. H **Pensión Kaia** (€35-45/55-80): , Puerto 12, 699821532
10. H **Pensión Donostiarra** (€37+/45+): , San Martín 6, 943426167
11. H **Pensión Artea** (€30+/45+): , San Bartolome 33, 943052780
12. H **Olarain** (€58-100/62-125): , Ondarreta Pasealekua 24, 943003300, near beach

San Sebastián

Doce Tribus and Ulia 5 6 →
Claret Ikastola 1
Zurriola
Nafarroa
Monte Urgull, 125m
San Telmo
Casco Viejo
Nicolosa 7
Kaia 9
8 Kati
Zurriola
Kolon
Bermingham
Aquarium
Isla de Santa Clara
Mirakruz
Alderdi Eder
Askatasunaren
Cable Car
Downtown River 3
Donostiarra 10
San Sebastián/Donostia
San Sebastián/Donostia
La Concha
Zubieta
San Martin
Buen Pastor
4 A Room in the City
Urbieta
Prim
Gernikako Arbola
Urumea
Igeldo
Satrustegi
Tunnel
De Zumalakarregi
11 Artea
Easo
2 La Sirena
← 12 Olarain
Aldapeta
Tolosa
Pío Baroja
Donostia
N
250m
0 125 250

2 SAN SEBASTIAN TO ZARAUTZ

21.5km (13.4mi), 5.5-8 HOURS, DIFFICULTY:

P 75%, 16.2km, U 25%, 5.3km

Begin with a steep climb out of San Sebastián, then ascend gradually to a high point (315m). Few services before San Martín (15.8km). Igueldo (5.2km) has private accommodations (H Buenavista has , but not always open). There's a spring with potable water (10.6km). After Orio, follow a road on the west side of the river with little traffic but almost no shoulder. Pilgrims who want to avoid this road can follow the dirt GR121 (walk just past thc paved road turn-off and go right on GR121). GR121 rejoins the Camino route 1.4km ahead, just past Albergue Txurruka (a youth hostel that does not host pilgrims).

5.2 Igueldo H Basque: *Igeldo*

H **Buenavista** (€45+/78+): , Kristobal Balentziaga 42, 943210600

H **Tximistarri** (€25-60): , Tximistarri 20, 943218801

H **Nicol's** (€45-70/70-117): , Gudamendi 21, 943215799, Mar-Nov, +700m

H **Agroturismo Maddiola** (€56/67+): , Aita Orkolaga 161, 652703128, +600m

15.8 San Martín A H / 16.4 Orio H Market 600m downhill in Orio.

1. A **San Martín** (20, €10): , La Ermita, 617118689, 2pm
2. H **Txanka Erreka** (€39+/58+): , San Martín 5, 943890535, 1.1km before Orio
3. H **Pensión Xaloa** (€46-57/61-83): , Estropalari 26, 943131883, +600m
4. H **Casa Rural Mailán** (€66-85): , Arratola 18, 943890345
5. H **Casa Rural Amalur** (€35-44): , Txanka Aldea 2, 943832888, +600m

Camping Playa de Orio (€10-17/tent): Hondartza Bidea, 943834801

21.5 Zarautz A H

1. A **Ebro-Extea** (muni, 60, don): , Zumalakarregi 16, July-Aug only
2. A H **Zarautz Hostel** (€22-35/-/50-70): , Gipuzkoa 59, 943833893
3. A **Galerna Zarautz Hostel** (16, €22): , Mitxelena 35, 943010371
4. H **Pensión Lagunak** (€30-50/35-65): , San Francisco 10, 943833701
5. H **Pensión Txiki Polit** (€35-65/45-80): , Musika Plaza, 943835357
6. H **Pensión Musika Plaza** (€30-80/35-85): , Nagusia 7, 943011159
7. H **Olatu** (€40-88/50-98): , Ipar Kalea 10, 943005522
8. H **Pensión Ekia** (€40-80/55-90): , Elizaurre 3, 943010664

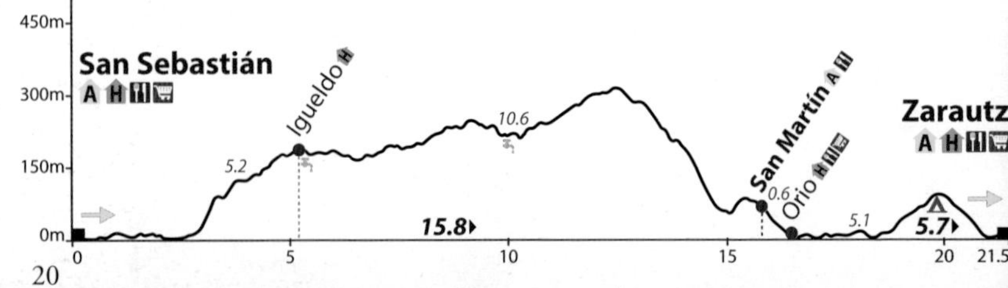

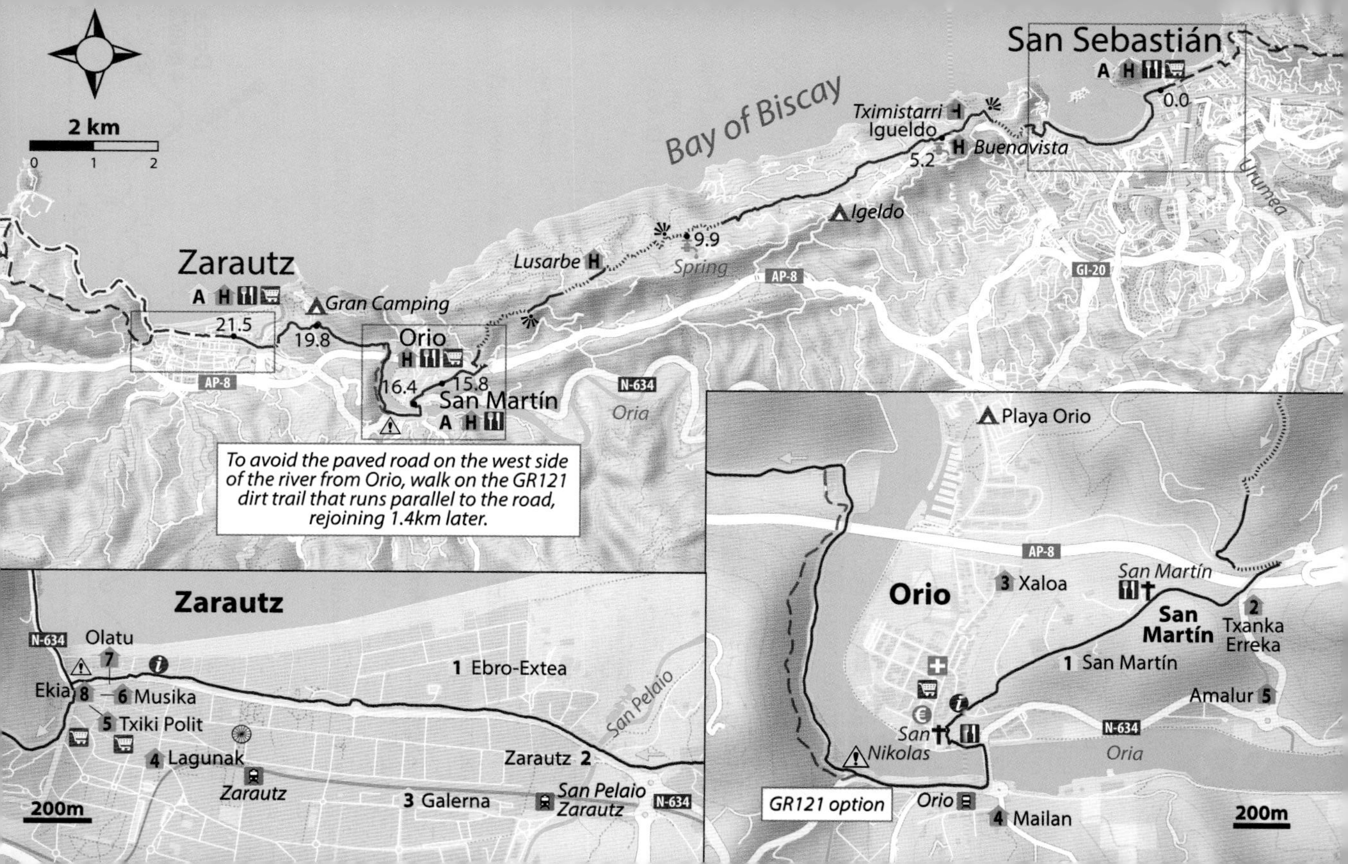

2 km
0
1
2
San Sebastián
0.0
Bay of Biscay
Tximistarri
Igueldo
Buenavista
5.2
Urumea
Igeldo
9.9
Spring
Lusarbe
GI-20
AP-8
Zarautz
Gran Camping
21.5
19.8
Orio
16.4
15.8
San Martín
N-634
Oria
To avoid the paved road on the west side of the river from Orio, walk on the GR121 dirt trail that runs parallel to the road, rejoining 1.4km later.
Zarautz
N-634
Olatu
7
Ekia
8
6 Musika
5 Txiki Polit
4 Lagunak
Zarautz
1 Ebro-Extea
San Pelaio
Zarautz 2
3 Galerna
San Pelaio Zarautz
N-634
200m
Playa Orio
AP-8
San Martín
3 Xaloa
Orio
San Martín
2
Txanka Erreka
1 San Martín
Amalur 5
N-634
Oria
San
Nikolas
GR121 option
Orio
4 Mailan
200m

3 ZARAUTZ TO DEBA

23.0km (14.3mi), 7-9 Hours, Difficulty:

P 75%, 17.2km, U 25%, 5.8km

From Zarautz, the route splits ❶ (Southern, recommended) climbs steeply to Santa Bárbara, with wonderful views, before descending to Getaria, ❷ (Northern, 0.2km shorter, much less climbing) follows a pedestrian way along the coast adjacent to N-634.

5.5 Getaria A H

1. A **Kanpaia** (30, €12): , Akerregui Auzoa, 695711679, Mar-O.
2. H **Pensión Getariano** (€40-75/55-95): , Herrerieta 3, 943140567
3. H **Itxas Gain Getaria** (€55/65): , San Roque 1, 943141035
4. H **Saiaz Getaria** (€75+): , Roque 25, 943140143
5. H **Pensión Iribar** (€50-70): , Aldamar 23, 943140451
6. H **Gaintza** (€72+): , San Prudentzio 26, 943140032

7.3 Askizu A: A **Agote Aundi** (15, €15): , 943140455, a.y.

10.7 Zumaia A H Most services are in center 0.5km before A.

1. A **Convento San José** (muni, 40, don): , Arritokieta, 943143396, 3pm Apr-Oct 15, 2-3 beds per room, in high season only for pilgrims who walked >15km
2. A H **Klara** (16, €25/35/60): , Sección 4, 943860531, a.y.
3. H **Pensión Goiko** (€30-40/40-60): , Erribera 9, 943860078
4. H **Hotel Zumaia** (€80+): , Alai Auzategia Auzoa 13, 943143441
5. H **Casa Rural Landarte** (€60-75/70-89): , Artadi 1, 943865358, +1km
6. H **Talasoterapia Zelai** (€75/99+): , Playa Itzurun, 943865100, seawater spa

19.5 Itziar H: H **Kanala** (€49+/59+): , Itziar Ind. 2, 943199035

H **Donibane** (€38-48/45-55): , Egia Auzoa, 617686337, 1.8km past Itziar

23.0 Deba A H Last until Markina-Xemein.

1. A **Geltoki** (56, €5): , Arakistain Plaza 3, 943192452, 4pm all year, former train station, register at i or if closed, local police 689125889
2. H **Pensión Zumardi** (€50-60/70-85): , Marina 12, 943192368

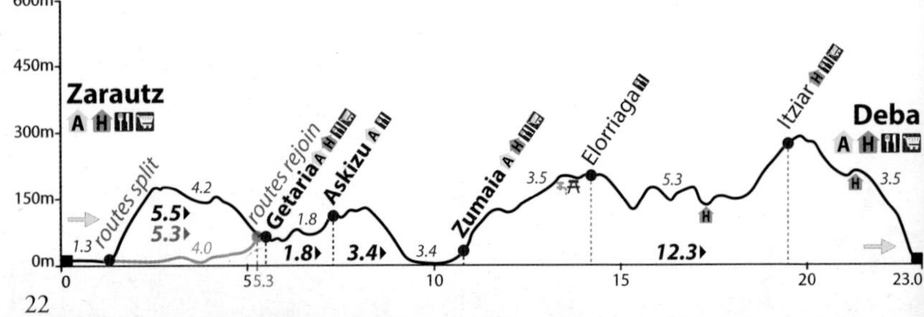

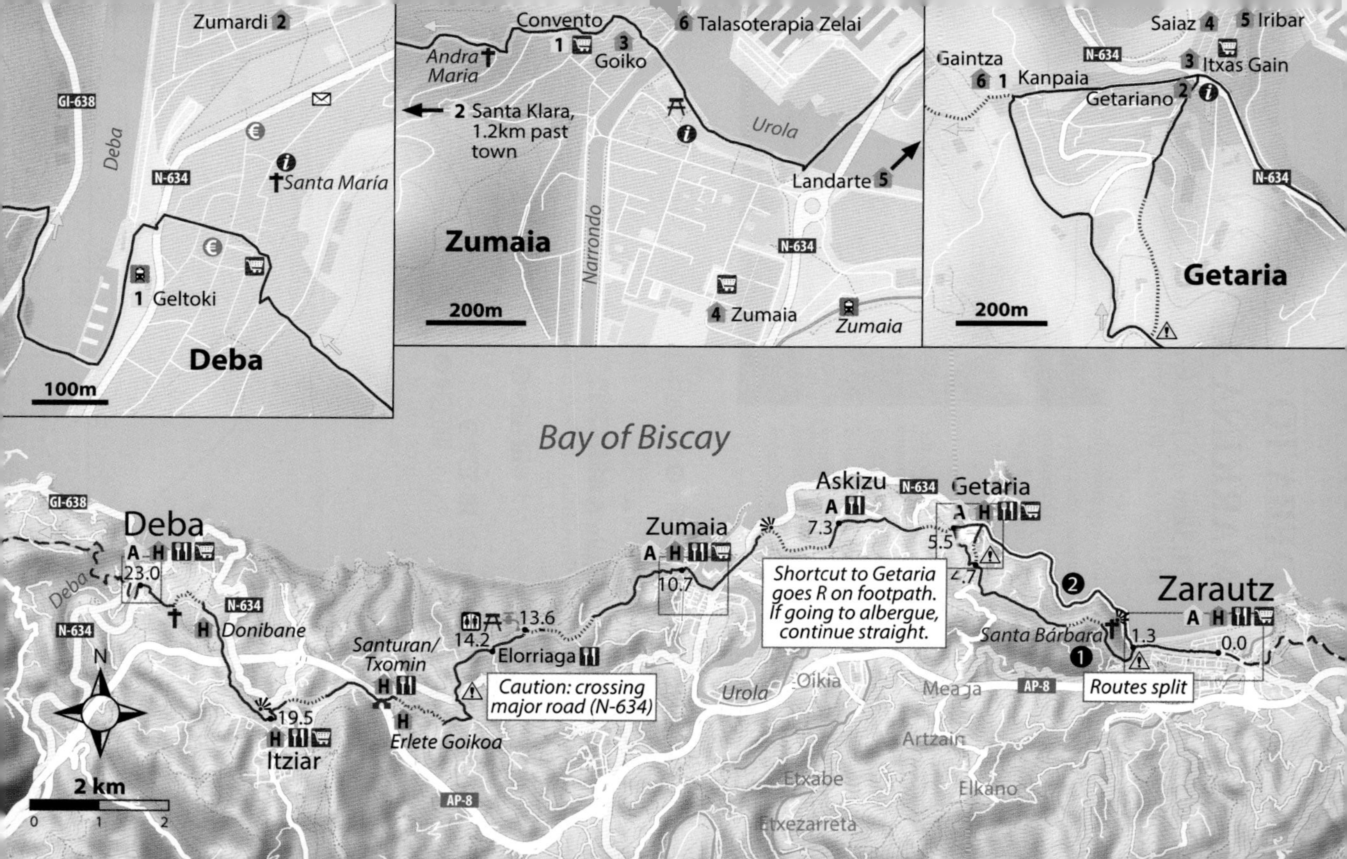
Zumardi 2
GI-638
Deba
N-634
Santa María
1 Geltoki
Deba
100m
Convento
1
3
Goiko
Andra María
6 Talasoterapia Zelai
2 Santa Klara, 1.2km past town
Urola
Landarte 5
Zumaia
Narrondo
N-634
200m
4 Zumaia
Zumaia
Gaintza
6 1 Kanpaia
N-634
Saiaz 4
5 Iribar
3 Itxas Gain
Getariano 2
N-634
Getaria
200m
Bay of Biscay
GI-638
Deba
23.0
Deba
N-634
N-634
Donibane
N
2 km
0
1
2
19.5
Itziar
Santuran/
Txomin
Erlete Goikoa
13.6
14.2
Elorriaga
Caution: crossing major road (N-634)
AP-8
Zumaia
10.7
Askizu
7.3
N-634
Getaria
5.5
4.7
Shortcut to Getaria goes R on footpath. If going to albergue, continue straight.
Urola
Oikia
Meaga
Artzain
Etxabe
Elkano
Etxezarreta
AP-8
Santa Bárbara
1.3
0.0
Zarautz
Routes split

4 DEBA TO MARKINA-XEMEIN

24.3km (15.1mi), 8-10 Hours, Difficulty:
P 34%, 8.2km, U 66%, 16.1km

Today the route leads away from the coast, up into more remote mountainous Basque countryside. The challenging climbs through beautiful forests and past quaint mountain farms lead to many expansive views!

There are few services—don't count on the restaurant by the Ermita de Calvario (3.9km) or the tavern in Olatz (7.7km) being open, so pack accordingly. A roofed spring at Arnoate (little more than a couple lone houses at a remote forested junction, 13.5km) provides a reliable potable water source.

4.8 Ibiri A

A Izarbide (32, €13): Ibiri Auzoa 3A, 655459769, Mar-Oct, dinner €12, breakfast €5, beautiful setting

24.3 Markina - Xemein A H

1. **A Convento Padres Carmelitas** (par, 40, don): Karmengo 5, 946166019, 3pm Apr-Oct 15
2. **A H Pitis** (12, €12-15/-/35): Karmengo 18, 657727824, all year, pilgrim menu €10
3. **A Augusto** (15, €15): Okerra Kalea 24, 667967555, 1pm a. y.
4. **A H Intxauspe** (12, €20/35/50): Barrio Atxondoa 10, 652770889 Mar-Nov, dinner €9.50, breakfast €3, very nice, +1km

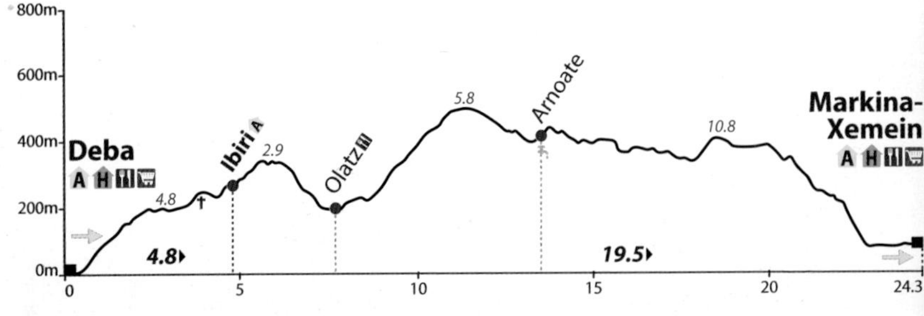

Markina-Xemein
BI-633
Artibai
San Miguel
Augusto
3
Par.
1
2 Pitis
Urko
Santa María
100m
Bay of Biscay
Ondarroa
Mijoa
Mutriku
GI-638
Calvario/Kalbaixo
Deba
A H
0.0
Ibiri
A
4.8
7.7
Olatz
N-634
AP-8
BI-633
21.9
24.3
Markina-Xemein
A H
13.5
Arnoate
N
2 km
0
1
2

5

MARKINA-XEMEIN TO GUERNICA

25.8km (16.0mi), **8-10 Hours, Difficulty:**

47%, 12.0km, 53%, 13.8km

Enjoy a pleasant day of hilly walking in rural countryside, through forests and near flowing streams. Follow the Artibai River, heading W, then S, to Iruzubieta and on to Bolibar. Climb to the beautiful Zenarruza monastery (wonderful A), before descending to Munitibar. The rest of the day passes through rolling terrain, much along footpaths following narrow streams.

6.3 Bolívar A Basque: *Bolibar*

A **Usandi** (20, €12): , Urezandi 3, 637054023, Mar-Oct

7.5 Zenarruza A H

1. A H **Ziortzabeitia** (50, €13/40/55): , Goierri 13, 946165722
2. A **Monasterio de Zenarruza** (par, 20, don): , 946164179, 3pm all year, peaceful with evening vespers and pilgrim blessing, monastery brews craft beer

11.6 Munitibar A H

1. A **Lea** (muni, 10, €15): , Herriko Plaza 3, 615721807
2. H **Garro** (€55/70): , Barrio Gerrikaitz, 946164136, 1.1km before Munitibar

17.8 Mendata A

A **Andiketxe** (20, €12): , Barrio Olabe 13, 946253150, all year

25.8 Guernica A H Considered the spiritual capital of the Basque people and site of an aerial bombings of civilians in 1937 in the Spanish Civil War, memorialized in Picasso painting. Peace & Euskal Herria museums offer pilgrim discounts.

1. A **Municipal** (35, don): , Zearreta Auzunea 11, 609031526, August only
2. A **Gernika Lumo** (youth hostel, 70, €18): , Kortezubi 9, 946126959, 1:30pm all year, crowded and more oriented toward youth
3. H **Akelarre Ostatua** (€38-43/48-56): , B. Kalea 5, 946270197
4. H **Boliña** (€40/50): , Barrenkale 3, 946250300
5. H **Gernika** (€66/86): , Carlos Gangoiti 17, 946250350

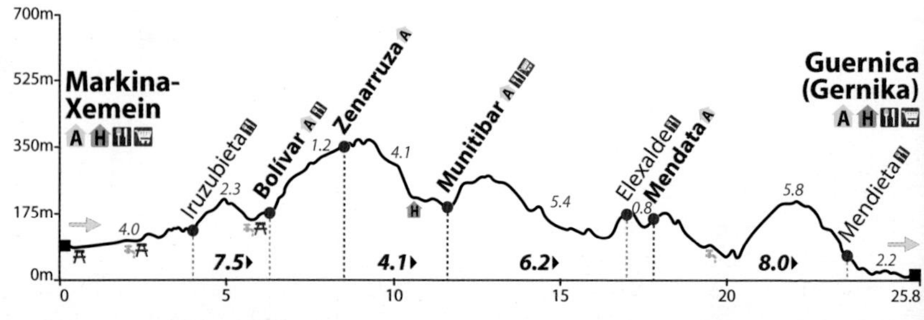

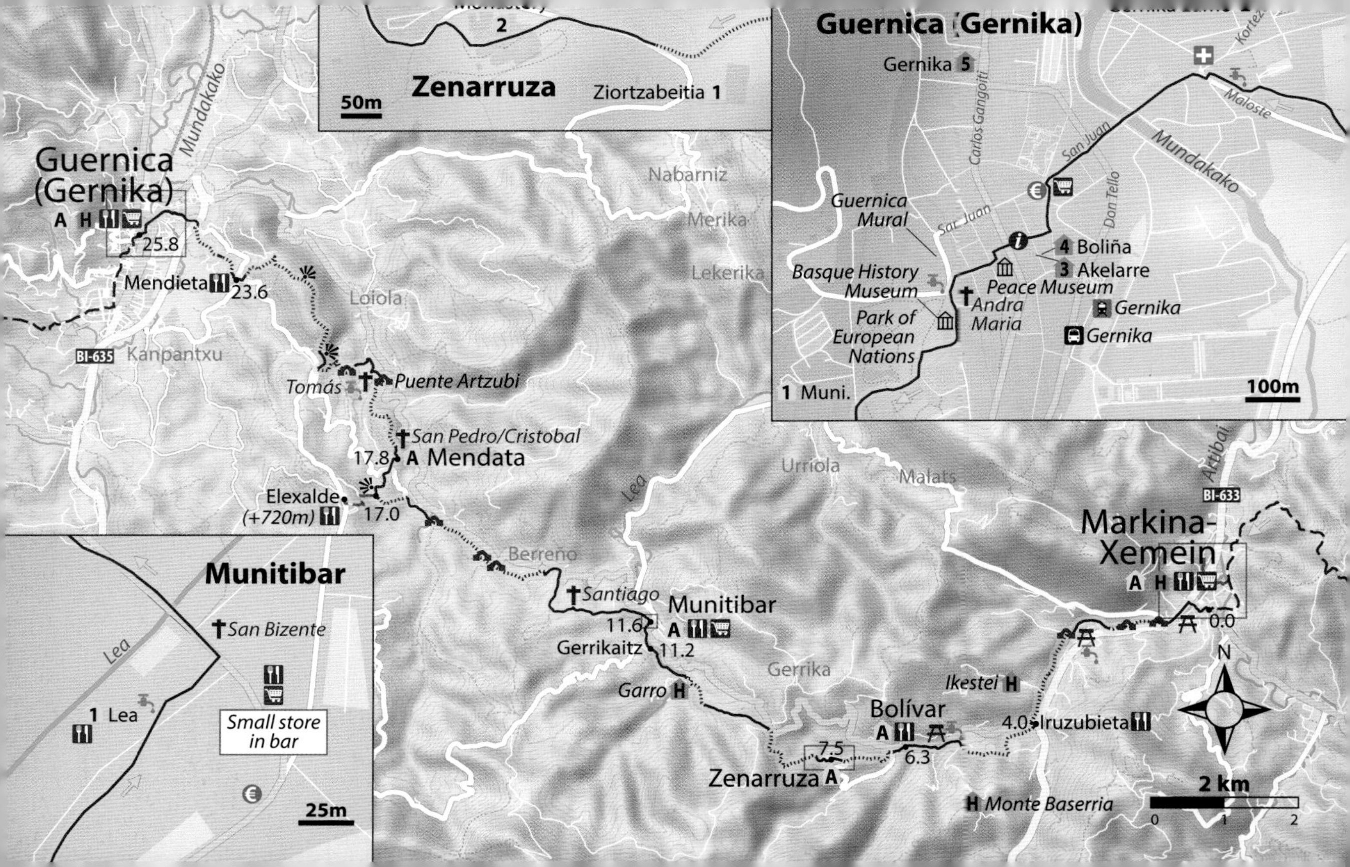

Guernica (Gernika)
25.8
Mendieta
23.6
Mundakako
BI-635
Kanpantxu
Loiola
Tomás
Puente Artzubi
San Pedro/Cristobal
17.8
Mendata
Elexalde
(+720m)
17.0
Nabarniz
Merika
Lekerika
Berreño
Lea
Santiago
Munitibar
11.6
Gerrikaitz
11.2
Garro
Gerrika
Urriola
Malats
Zenarruza
7.5
Bolívar
6.3
Ikestei
4.0
Iruzubieta
Monte Baserria
Markina-Xemein
0.0
Artibai
BI-633
N
2 km
0
1
2
Zenarruza
2
Ziortzabeitia 1
50m
Guernica (Gernika)
Gernika 5
Carlos Gangoiti
San Juan
Don Tello
Mundakako
Maloste
Kortez
Guernica Mural
Basque History Museum
Park of European Nations
Andra Maria
Peace Museum
4 Boliña
3 Akelarre
Gernika
Gernika
1 Muni.
100m
Munitibar
San Bizente
Lea
1 Lea
Small store in bar
25m

6 GUERNICA TO LARRABETZU

16.5km (10.3mi), **5-6.5 Hours, Difficulty:**

P 59%, 9.7km, U 41%, 6.8km

While relatively short, this stage has a significant amount of climbing. If the distance feels too short, the walk to Bilbao (to the Santiago Cathedral, in the Casco Viejo on the eastern side of the city) is 30.8km. Continuing to the A municipal in Bilbao adds another 4.4km. Once again, the Camino passes through picturesque rural countryside.

5.5 A **Pozueta** (5, €14): , Pozueta Auzoa 5, 696565318, all year

9.6 **Eskerica** A H A, Basque: *Eskerika*

A H A **Eskerika** (22, €14/-/50, A €5/tent + €5/person): , Eskerika Auzoa 10, 696453582, 3pm late Mar-mid Nov, +300m, isolated farmhouse, recommended to bring food for dinner, basic supplies at the A, use of €1, €2

16.5 **Larrabetzu** A The albergue is located in the town square. Cafés and a grocery store are all located within a radius of 200m.

A **Municipal** (20, don): , A. Enparantza 1, 609031526, 3pm Apr-Sep

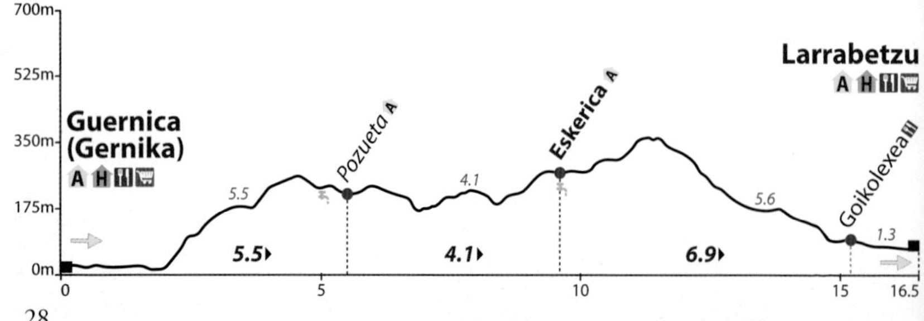

Guernica
(Gernika)
A H
0.0
Butron
Iberbur
Fika
Meakaur
Errigoiti
Mikiene
Santa Luiza
Mundakako
5.5
A
Pozueta
San Esteban
Oñarte
Morga
Kanpantxu
BI-635
Amunaga
Muxika
Eskerika
+300m A
9.6
Alto, 364m
Aretxabalgane
Mundaka
Goikolexea
15.2
16.5
BI-737
Larrabetzu
A
N-637
N
1 km
0
0.5
1

7 LARRABETZU TO BILBAO

14.3km (8.9mi), 4-5.5 Hours, Difficulty:

P 90%, 12.9km, U 10%, 1.4km

The scenery becomes decidedly more urban and mundane approaching Bilbao, although the climb to Mt. Avril offers a nice break from city walking. At the crest of the pass at the entrance to Mt. Avril Park, you can detour left from the Camino to reach a wonderful viewpoint that overlooks Bilbao. Shortly after crossing the pass, there's a picnic area with potable water, perfect for a lunch break.

The stage ends at the Santiago Cathedral in the Old City, but depending on where you're staying and your interest in exploring the city, you may add a few more kilometers to your day. The municipal albergue is located on a hill on the western edge of town and is 4.4km past the cathedral. If you prefer a more central location, Bilbao has many accommodations options, including two other pilgrim-oriented albergues. This shorter walking stage may allow you some time to take in the sites of Bilbao, such as the famous modern art museum, Guggenheim Bilbao (Tues-Sun 10am-8pm, €16). Bilbao city map and lodging on next page.

3.3 Lezama A H

1. A **Centro Uribarri Topalekua** (muni, 20, don): M W D, Garaioltza 133E, 944556007, 3-10pm Jun-Sept, extra 20 in August
2. H **Madarian** (€55-58/62-68): , Aretxalde 88, 944554427, +700m, €6
3. H **Matsa** (€66/83): , Aretxalde 153, 944556086, 1.5km after Lezama, +700m

6.4 Zamudio H

H **Aretxarte** (€66+/70+): , Parque Tecnológico de Zamudio 200, 944036900, +700m

H **Casa Rural Iabiti** (€67/75): K, Arteaga Auzoa 13, 944522370

Continued on next page

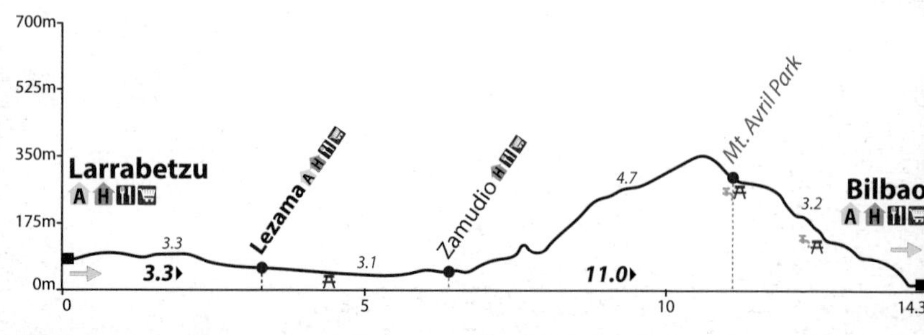

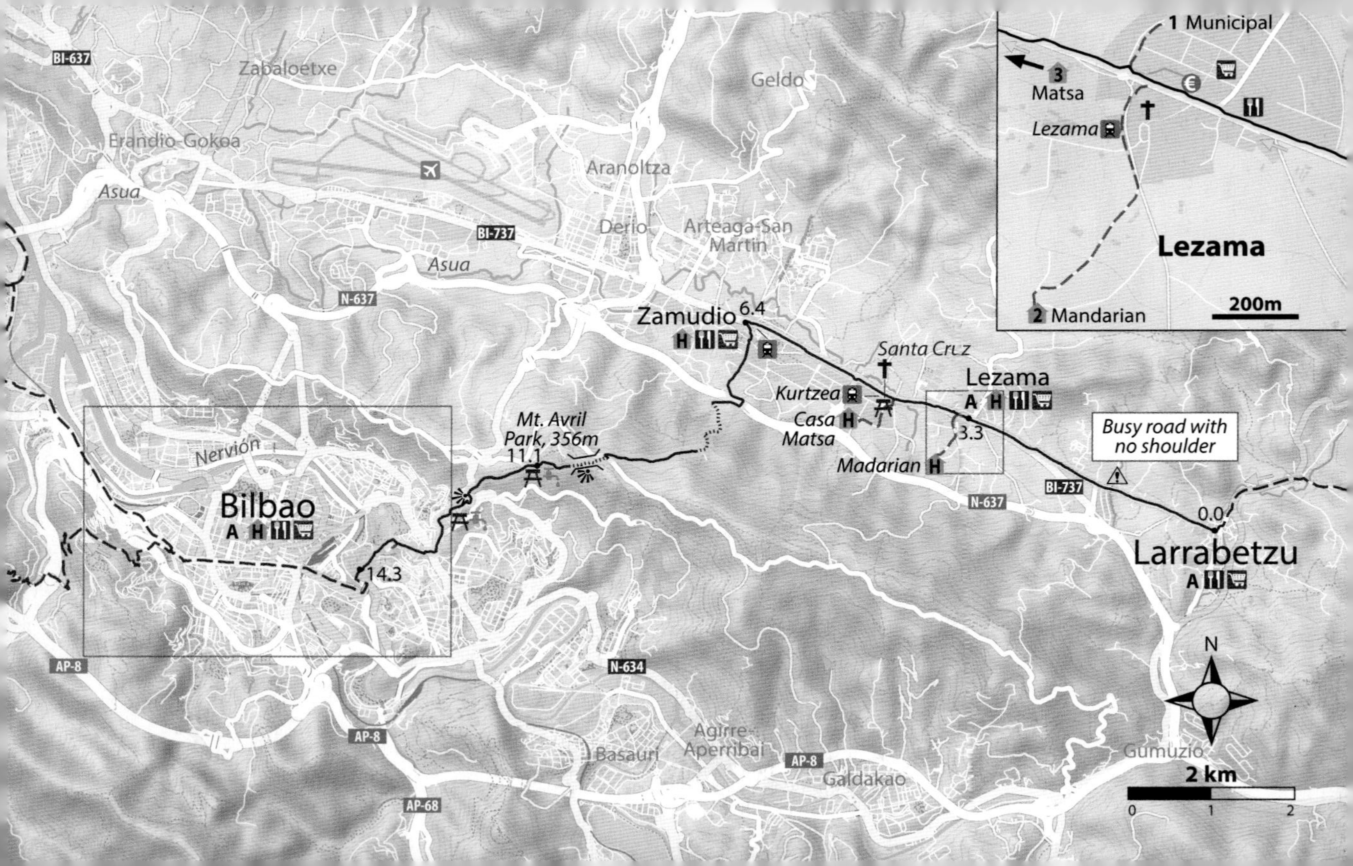
1 Municipal
3 Matsa
Lezama
Lezama
200m
2 Mandarian
BI-637
Zabaloetxe
Geldo
Erandio-Gokoa
Aranoltza
Asua
Derio
Arteaga-San Martin
BI-737
Asua
N-637
Zamudio 6.4
H
Santa Cruz
Lezama
A H
Kurtzea
Casa Matsa H
Busy road with no shoulder
Mt. Avril Park, 356m
11.1
3.3
Madarian H
Nervión
Bilbao
A H
BI-737
N-637
0.0
Larrabetzu
A
14.3
AP-8
N-634
N
AP-8
Agirre-Aperribai
Basauri
AP-8
Gumuzio
Galdakao
2 km
0
1
2
AP-68

14.3 Bilbao

1. Municipal (Altamira) (40, don): Kobeta 60, 609031526, 3pm April-mid Oct, bus 58 to downtown, 4.4km after city center on longer route from Bilbao
2. Santa Cruz de Begoña (par, 20, don): Padre Remigio Vilariño 1, 687529627, 3pm 15 June - 15 Sept
3. Claret Enea (20, €11): Plaza Corazón de María, 609087620, 3pm May-Oct, run by charity in a space also used as a winter homeless shelter
4. All Iron Hostel (84, €17+): Jose María Ugarteburn 2, 944036534, all year
5. Ganbara Hostel (62, €18-22): all year, Prim 13, 944053930, close to old city
6. Quartier Bilbao (34, €18+): Artekale 15, 944978800
7. Bilbao Central Hostel (56, €17+): Fernández del Campo 24, 946526057, central location close to bus station
8. Pil Pil (62, €19+/55/75): Sabino Arana Etorbidea 14, 944345544
9. Juvenil de Bilbao (youth hostel, 142, €19-23/-/50): Basurto Kastrexana 70, 944270054, all year
10. Akelarre Hostel (38, €15-20): Morgan 4-6, 944057713, youth oriented
11. Moon Hostel Bio (90, €9-15/30/35): Luzarra 7, 944750848
12. BBK (106, €17-21/-/45-70): Miraflores 16, 944597759, all year, +1.8km, 10% pilgrim discount
13. BCool Bilbao (122, €17-24/-/68-88): Hernani 19, 946066200
14. Méndez I Boarding House (€30/40): Santa María 13, 944160364
15. 7Kale (€60-100/70-120): Santa María 13, 946402011
16. Bilbao Jardines (€55+/85+): Jardines 9, 944794210
17. Bilbao Art Lodge (€80/115+): Iturriza Kalea 3, 946855951

Bilbao
11 Moon
Agirre Lehendakariaren
Madariaga
Blas de Otero
Walking Bridge
Unibertsitate
10 Akelarre
Botikazar
Guggenheim Museum
Plaza
Euskadi
Mazarredo
Museum of Fine Arts
Parque de
Doña Casilda
Nervión
Uribitarte
Juan Ajuriaguerra
Henao
Colón de Larreátegui
Diego López
Aguirre
Rodríguez Arias
Sabino Arana
Plaza
Mouya
Parque
Etxebarria
BI-625
A-8
9
Juvenil
Pil Pil 8
Máximo
Iparraguirre
Altamira
Municipal
1
N-634
Simón Bolivar
Ukrixo
Alameda de Recalde
Areilza Doktorearen
Basurto/Hospital
Hurtado de Amézaga
All
Iron
4
Virgen de
Begoña
7 Central
Fernández
Kale 15
Méndez I
Jardines 16
14
2 Santa
5 Cruz
Begoña
17 Art Lodge
Ganbara
Basque Museum
Santiago
Autonomia
Ferrocarril
BCool
13
Convent
3
6 Quartier
Gorte
Claret
Enea
San Frantzisko
N-634
A-8
N
500m
0
250
500
BBK 12

8 BILBAO TO POBEÑA

31.9km (19.8mi), 9.5-12 HOURS, DIFFICULTY:

P 92%, 29.2km, U 8%, 2.7km

Two marked options leaving Bilbao split just before the Basurto/Hospital train stop west of Bilbao. ❶ (Recommended) climbs to the municipal albergue on a ridge above Bilbao before descending on dirt tracks to the Cadagua River and town of Castrejana. After crossing the Cadagua on the Puente del Diablo and passing a junction with a Camino route that returns to the Camino Francés in Burgos, ascend to the Santa Águeda church. Enjoy spectacular views and pass through working class neighborhoods above Bilbao en route to Barakaldo and Sestao. ❷ Generally follows the Nervión River—initially following highway N-634 and later on smaller roads and paved pedestrian paths—meeting the first route just before Sestao. This option is flatter and 6.2km shorter but is mostly unpleasant urban walking. If you have the time, take the first option. The extra distance and climbing pay off with exceptional views around Santa Águeda. Portugalete also makes a good overnight stop, with a manageable day to Ontón (17.9km) or Castro-Urdiales (27.3km) to follow.

13.7 **Barakaldo** A H

A **Polideportivo Gorostiza** (muni, 16, don): , 944789906, 3pm June-Sept, call to check latest status and open dates, adjacent to park 1.8km before Barakaldo, accessible only from ❶ route option, housed in sports center

H **Hostal Retuerto** (€30/40): Noberto Acebal 2, 944956296

H **Pensión Zeus** (€45/60): , Telleria 10, 944996100

19.9 **Portugalete** A H Note the unique transporter bridge, which is a World Heritage site. Bilbao's metro reaches Portugalete. From Portugalete, a paved bike path crosses AP-8 and continues to Playa de Arena, passing several nice picnic areas. Portugalete has the last real shop until Castro Urdiales, so stock up accordingly.

1. A **Municipal** (30, don): , Martin F. Villaran 2, 944729314, 3pm Jun-Sep
2. A **Bide Ona** (34, €12+): , J. G. Lumbreras 10, 946038630, a. y.
3. H **Pensión Santa María** (€25-36/35-42): , Salcedo 1, 944722489
4. H **Pensión La Guía** (€22-30/32-40): Virgen de la Guía 4, 944837530, +800m
5. H **Pensión Buenavista** (€20/30): San Juan Bautista 1, 944044644

Continued on map

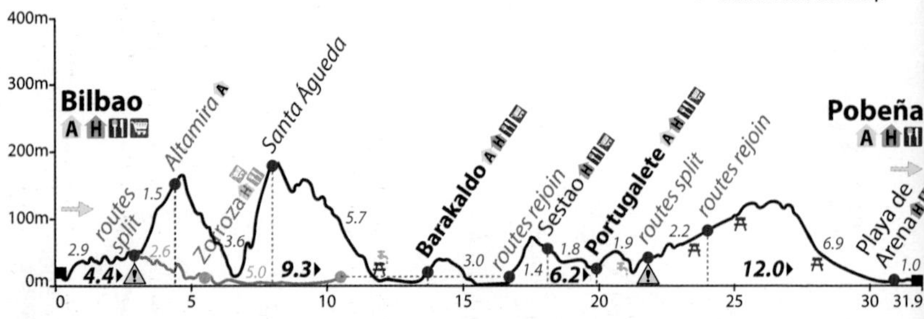

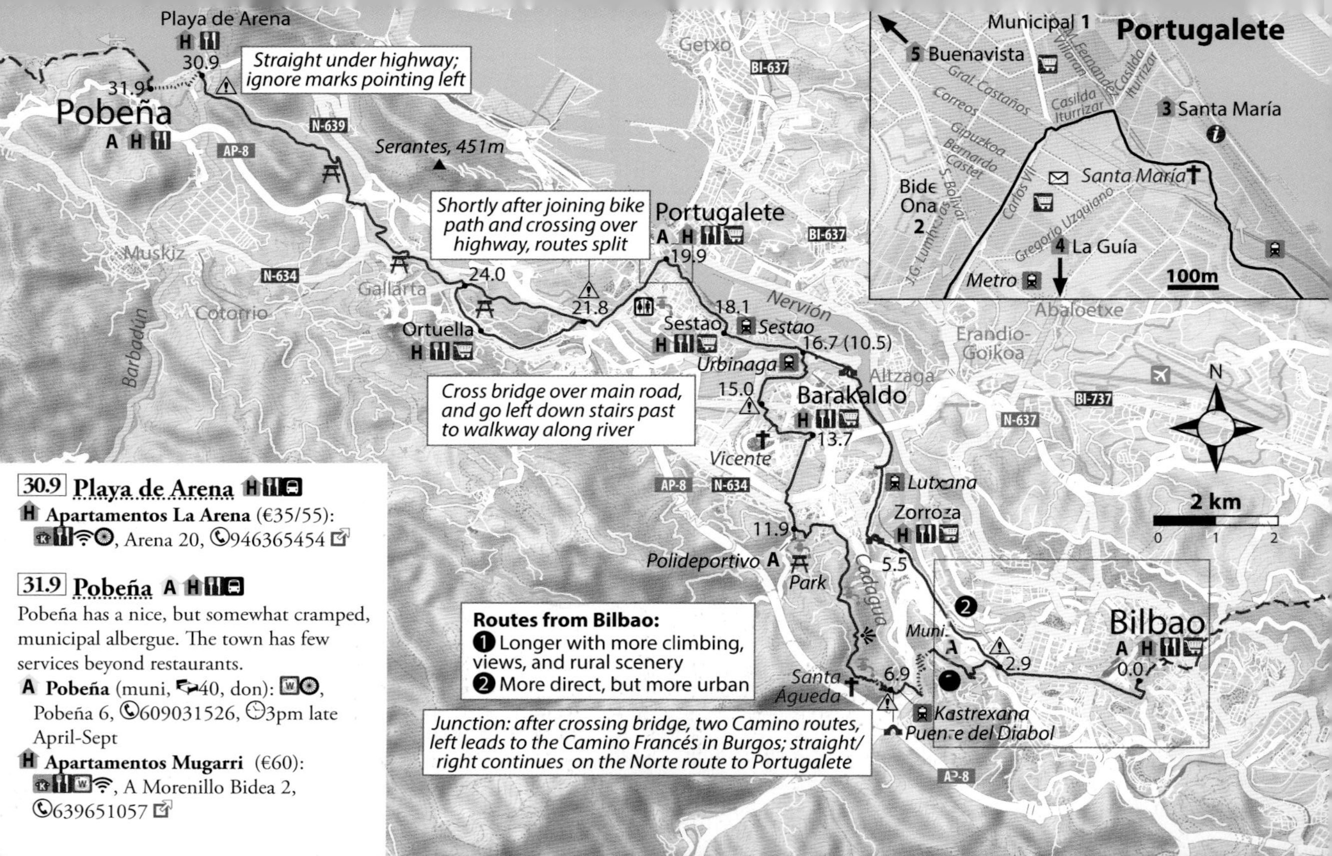

30.9 **Playa de Arena**

H Apartamentos La Arena (€35/55): , Arena 20, 946365454

31.9 **Pobeña** A H

Pobeña has a nice, but somewhat cramped, municipal albergue. The town has few services beyond restaurants.

A Pobeña (muni, 40, don): , Pobeña 6, 609031526, 3pm late April-Sept

H Apartamentos Mugarri (€60): , A Morenillo Bidea 2, 639651057

9 POBEÑA TO CASTRO-URDIALES

15.3km (9.5mi), 4.5-5.5 Hours, Difficulty:
P 91%, 13.9km, U 9%, 1.4km

From Pobeña's **A**, return to the Camino route, climb a set of stairs, and enjoy a splendid section of walking on a pedestrian path that runs along the coastline above the ocean. Once in Ontón, the route splits with ⚠ **two options to Castro Urdiales.** ❶ The first is 8km shorter and closer to the coast. Climbing out of Ontón, descend to Mioño, on N-634 the whole way (⚠ traffic)! Just after Mioño, go through a tunnel to the outskirts of Castro Urdiales. ❷ The second (mountain views) leaves south from Ontón, climbing to a pass (254m). After descending, follow a bike path to Santullán (great views of Peña de Santullán). Continue on mostly residential roads, joining the main route before Castro Urdiales. Say goodbye to Basque Country today—once you reach Ontón, you've arrived in Cantabria.

5.9 Ontón A H Hotel and restaurant +1.2km off route.
A Tu Camino (asoc, 25, €6): , N-634 71, 645985269, 2pm all year
H El Haya (€45/80): , N-634 km 137, 942879306, +1.2km

10.5 Mioño H
H Mioño Hotel Suite (€42-50/55-69): , Crta Mioño-Lusa, 942879555

15.3 Castro-Urdiales A H Historic town with scenic harbor

1. **A Municipal** (16+, €5): , Barrio Urdiales 2041, 620608118, 3:30pm all year call in winter, extra beds in tents in summer, fills early, 1.4km after town center
2. **H Pensión La Mar** (€35-48/52-65): , La Mar 27, 942870524
3. **H Pensión Ardigales 11** (€42-56/58-78): , Ardigales 11, 942781616
4. **H La Marina** (€24/34 shared bath): , Plazuela 16, 942861345, mixed reviews
5. **H La Ronda** (€40-50/55-66): , La Ronda 18, 942864040
6. **H Pensión Chili** (€35+/45+): , La Ronda 16, 692846579
7. **H Hostal Catamarán** (€29-65/39-73): Victorina Gainza 3, 942784137
8. **H Hostería Villa de Castro** (€47-60/53-80): , Huertos 2, 650483650
9. **H Sercotel Las Rocas** (€76-135+): Flaviobriga 1, 902141515
10. **H Agua Viva & Spa Castro** (29+/39-59): , Alto Cruz 6, 942862238

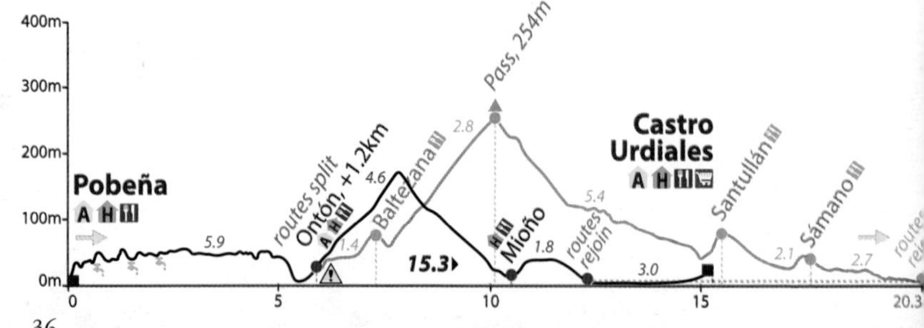

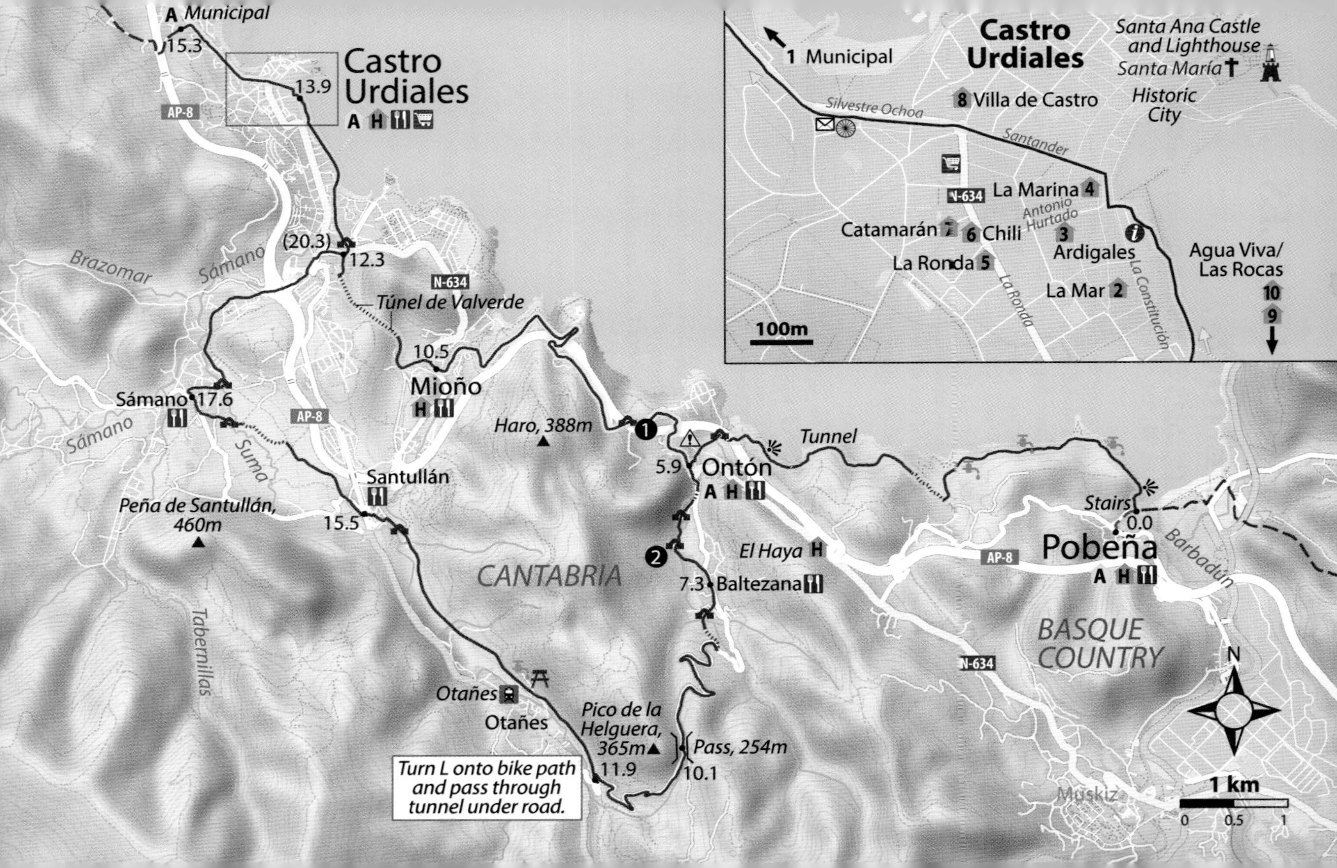
Castro Urdiales
1 Municipal
Santa Ana Castle and Lighthouse
Santa María
Historic City
8 Villa de Castro
Silvestre Ochoa
Santander
N-634
La Marina 4
Antonio Hurtado
Catamarán 7
6 Chili
3 Ardigales
La Ronda 5
La Mar 2
La Ronda
La Constitución
Agua Viva/ Las Rocas
10
9
100m
Municipal
15.3
13.9
Castro Urdiales
AP-8
(20.3)
12.3
Brazomar
Sámano
N-634
Túnel de Valverde
10.5
Mioño
Sámano
17.6
Suma
Santullán
Peña de Santullán, 460m
15.5
Haro, 388m
1
5.9
Ontón
Tunnel
Stairs
0.0
Pobeña
Barbadún
El Haya
2
7.3
Baltezana
CANTABRIA
BASQUE COUNTRY
N-634
Otañes
Otañes
Pico de la Helguera, 365m
Pass, 254m
11.9
10.1
Turn L onto bike path and pass through tunnel under road.
Muskiz
N
1 km
0
0.5
1

10 CASTRO-URDIALES TO LIENDO

24.4km (15.2mi), 7-9 Hours, Difficulty:
P 71%, 17.4km, U 29%, 7.0km

An enjoyable day of walking that begins along the coast before turning inland, eventually climbing on dirt roads through eucalyptus forests to quaint Liendo. We've split the Castro Urdiales-Güemes section (60.5km) into three stages (Castro Urdiales-Liendo; Liendo-Helgueras; Helgueras-Güemes), but many pilgrims walk to Güemes in two longer days: Castro Urdiales-Laredo (31.2km) and Laredo-Güemes (29.3km). In this configuration, some pilgrims shorten the day from Güemes to Laredo by following N-634 all the way to Laredo; in our opinion, this cuts out some of the nicest sections of the route before (remote forest and rural scenery) and after (rugged coastal views) Liendo. Albergues in El Pontarrón, and Santoña also make it easy to split up this section in any number of ways.

8.2 Islares A H

1. A **Municipal** (18, €8): , 671995870, **temporarily closed, may not reopen**
2. A **CaféBar Elisa** (5, €15): , Riego 78, 687415167, a. y., closed Thurs
3. H **Arenillas Hotel** (€31-35/50-60): , Islares 155, 942860766

Camping Playa Arenillas (€17+): , Barrio Arenillas 43, 942863152

11.6 El Pontarrón A

Not on official route, but a simple bypass goes past the town's café and albergue before coming back to the main route without extra distance.

A **Municipal** (14, don): , CA-151, 942850061, keys at café, mixed reviews

13.3 Rioseco H

H **Posada Fernanda** (€32/45): , 942850315/629457769

24.4 Liendo A H

Quiet, has all services a pilgrim needs.

1. A **Saturnino Candina** (18, €8): , Barr. Hazas 10, 682074723, good reviews
2. H **Posada la Torre de la Quintana** (€72): , Barrio de Hazas 26, 942677439
3. H **Pensión Bisabuela Martina** (€48-75): , 669147387

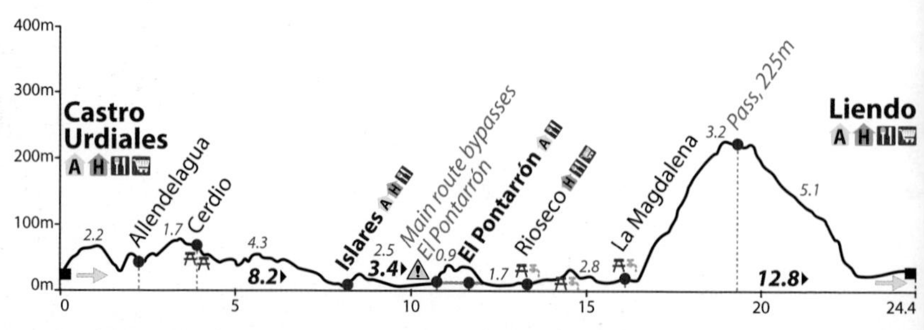

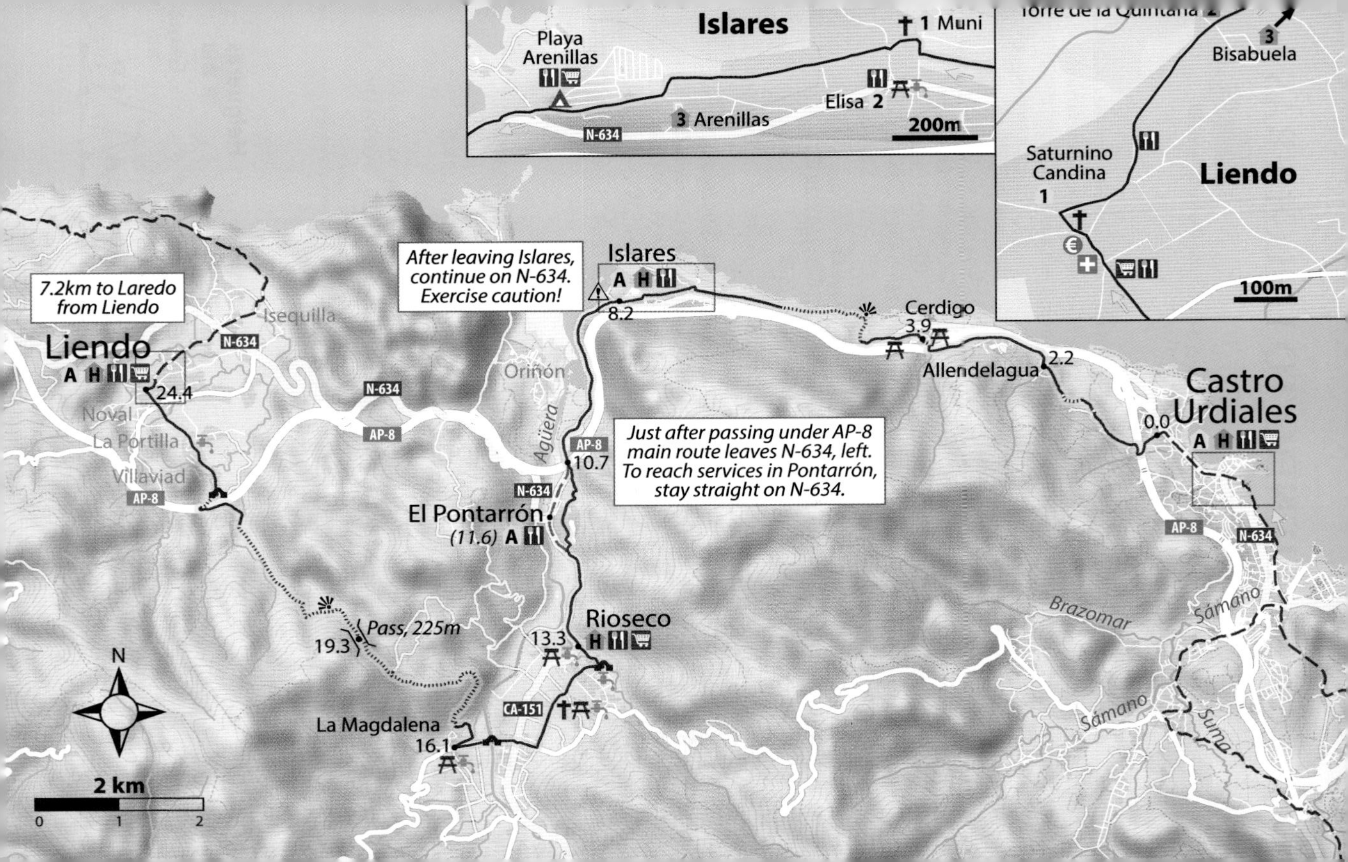

Islares
Playa Arenillas
1 Muni
Elisa 2
3 Arenillas
N-634
200m
Bisabuela
Saturnino Candina
1
Liendo
100m
7.2km to Laredo from Liendo
Liendo
A H
24.4
Isequilla
N-634
Noval
La Portilla
Villaviad
AP-8
N-634
AP-8
After leaving Islares, continue on N-634. Exercise caution!
Islares
A H
8.2
Oriñón
Agüera
AP-8
10.7
N-634
El Pontarrón
(11.6) A
Just after passing under AP-8 main route leaves N-634, left. To reach services in Pontarrón, stay straight on N-634.
Cerdigo
3.9
Allendelagua
2.2
Castro Urdiales
0.0
A H
AP-8
N-634
Brazomar
Sámano
Sámano
Suma
Rioseco
H
13.3
CA-151
La Magdalena
16.1
Pass, 225m
19.3
N
2 km
0
1
2

11 LIENDO TO HELGUERAS

19.2km (11.9mi), 5.5-7 Hours, Difficulty:
P 71%, 13.7km, U 29%, 5.5km

Follow dirt paths above the rugged coastline to Laredo (sections pass drop-offs—be careful in fog). Ferry to Santoña (€2, 675874742) operates 9am-9pm July/Aug, hours vary other months; no ferry Dec-Feb when the only option is ❷ inland via Gama.

7.2 Laredo A H

1. A **Buen Pastor** (20, €13): Fuente Fresnedo 1, 942606288, all year
2. A **Trinidad** (48, €12-21): S. Francisco 22, 639053072, 12pm a. y.
3. H **Pensión Esmeralda** (€25/34): Fuente Fresnedo 4, 942605219
4. H **Ramona** (€30-34/38-48): W D, España 4, 942607189, Mar-Oct
5. H **Tucán:** Gutiérrez Rada 2, 942607053
6. H **Cortijo** (€54/65): González Gallego 3, 942605600
7. H **Cosmopol** (€65+/90+): W D, Cantabria 27, 942605720
8. H **Carro** (€40/45): Barrio La Arenosa, 942606175

12.7 Santoña A H

1. A **Bilbaina** (40, €12): W D, Plaza San Antonio 1, 942661952, a. y.
2. A **Santoña** (youth hostel, 68, €9): Cicero 1, 942662008, a. y.
3. H **Hospedaje La Tortuga** (€48-70/65-108): Juan de la Cosa 39, 942683035
4. H **Alojamiento Buciero** (€40-60/55-80): W D, Manzanedo 1, 653986544
5. H **Miramar** (€40-55/45-60): W D, General Santiago 23, 942663130
6. H **Hostal El Parque:** El Cantal 15, 942662198

16.1 Playa de Berria H

H **Juan de la Cosa** (€60/65+): W D, Playa de Berria 14, 942661238
H **Hostal Berria** (€40-50/60-70): Playa Berria 40, 942660847, mixed reviews
H **Posada las Garzas** (€45-69/57-89): Primera Avenida 31, 942663484

19.2 Helgueras A H

More services in Noja (+1.8km, map on stage 12).

1. A H **Noja Aventura** (94, €10/25/40): W D, Helgueras 20, 609043397, 12pm all year, oriented toward surfing and water sports, mixed reviews

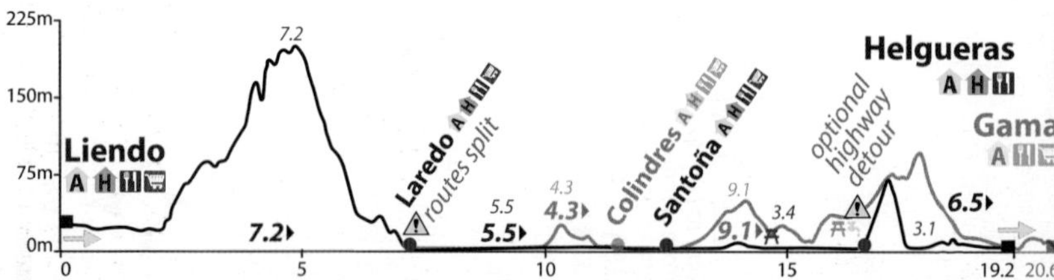

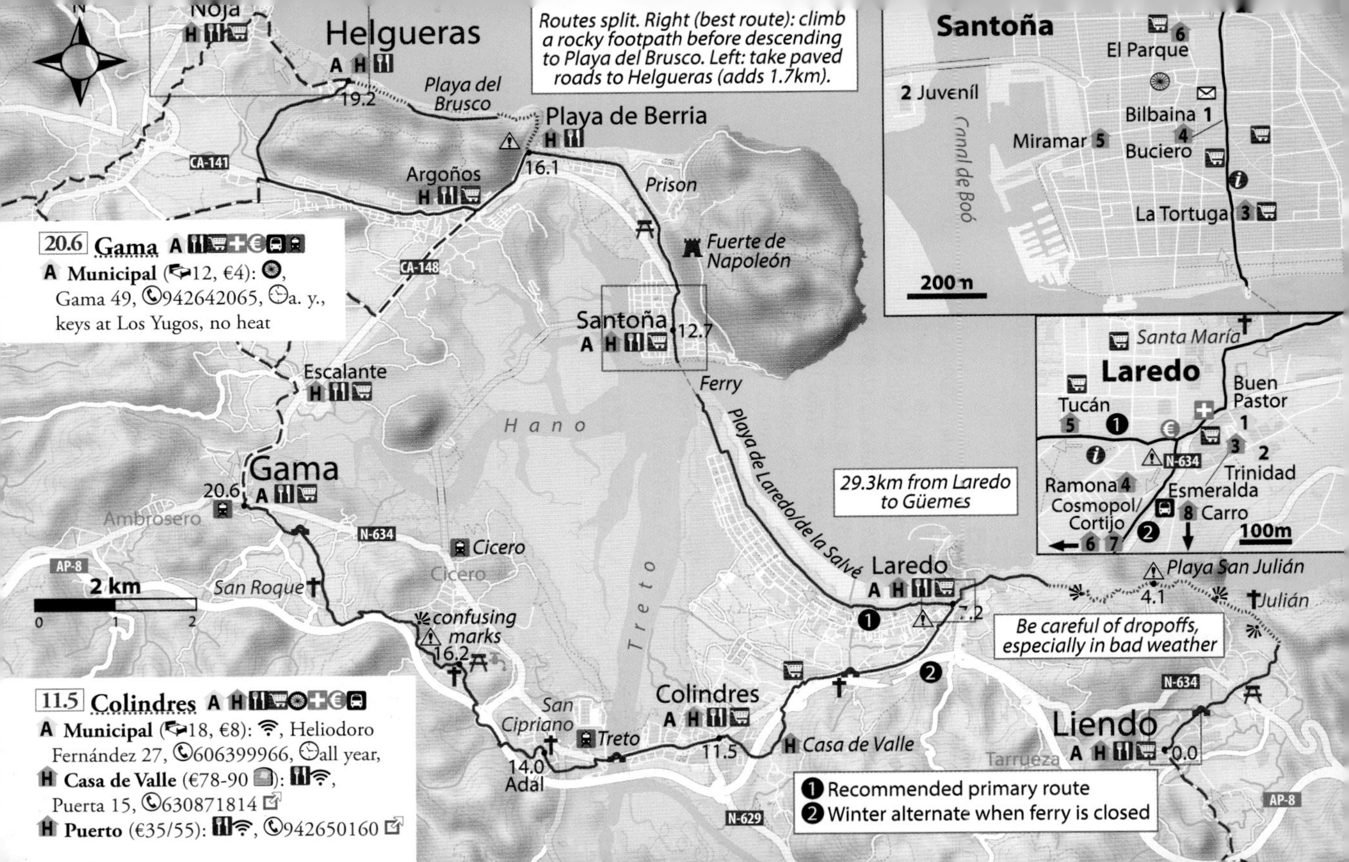

20.6 **Gama** A

A **Municipal** (12, €4): , Gama 49, 942642065, a. y., keys at Los Yugos, no heat

11.5 **Colindres** A H

A **Municipal** (18, €8): , Heliodoro Fernández 27, 606399966, all year,

H **Casa de Valle** (€78-90): , Puerta 15, 630871814

H **Puerto** (€35/55): , 942650160

12 HELGUERAS TO GÜEMES

16.8km (10.4mi), **4.5-6 Hours, Difficulty:**
P 94%, 15.8km, U 6%, 1.0km

Discerning the "official" route can be confusing with various options and unclear markings. ❶ **From Helgueras/Noja:** Continue on Playa Tregandín to Noja. Follow clear → SW on residential roads to CA-141 and Castillo. From there, → continue clearly to A Cabaña del Abuelo Peuto—one of the most meaningful pilgrim experiences of the entire route!

1.8 Noja

2. H **Arillo** (€55/65+): , Trengandin 6, 942630080
3. H **Las Olas** (€120/150+): , Trengandín 4, 942630036
4. H **La Casona** (€30+/45+): , Plaza de la Villa, 942631398
5. H **Posada La Míes** (€50-75): , Panadería 12, 942628809
6. H **María del Mar** (€45+/65+): , Panadería 20, 942630037
7. H **Hostería Los Laureles** (€58-85): , Viñas 14, 942630000
8. H **Hostelería Las Viñas** (€55-85): , Viñas 55, 942628890
9. H **Azcona** (€55+): Arco 26, 942630359
10. H **Pensión Dorada** (€48+): , Ris 60, 942630043

4.3 Castillo Siete Villas Eroski 200m east on CA-141.

H **Las Torres** (€60): , Barrio San Pantaleón 23, 942657129

8.6 San Miguel de Meruelo Services off route in center.

H **Hosteria Sol** (€30+/40+): , La Maza 43, 617729962, +500m

16.8 Güemes

A **Cabaña del Abuelo Peuto** (80, don): , Albergue 323, 942621122, started by enigmatic Camino character Padre Ernesto Bustio, when present he tells the story of the A and his travels and peace work in a moving evening ritual, by donation

H **Posada Valle de Güemes** (€100-150): , Pomero 103, 609480553

H **El Ángel de la Guarda Inn** (€70-100): , Barrio de la Iglesia, 942621038

H **CR Camino del Norte** (€40-60): Barcena 305, 638516191

Continued on map

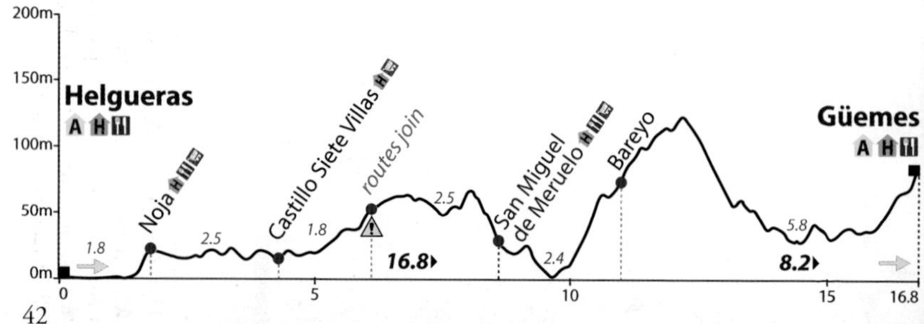

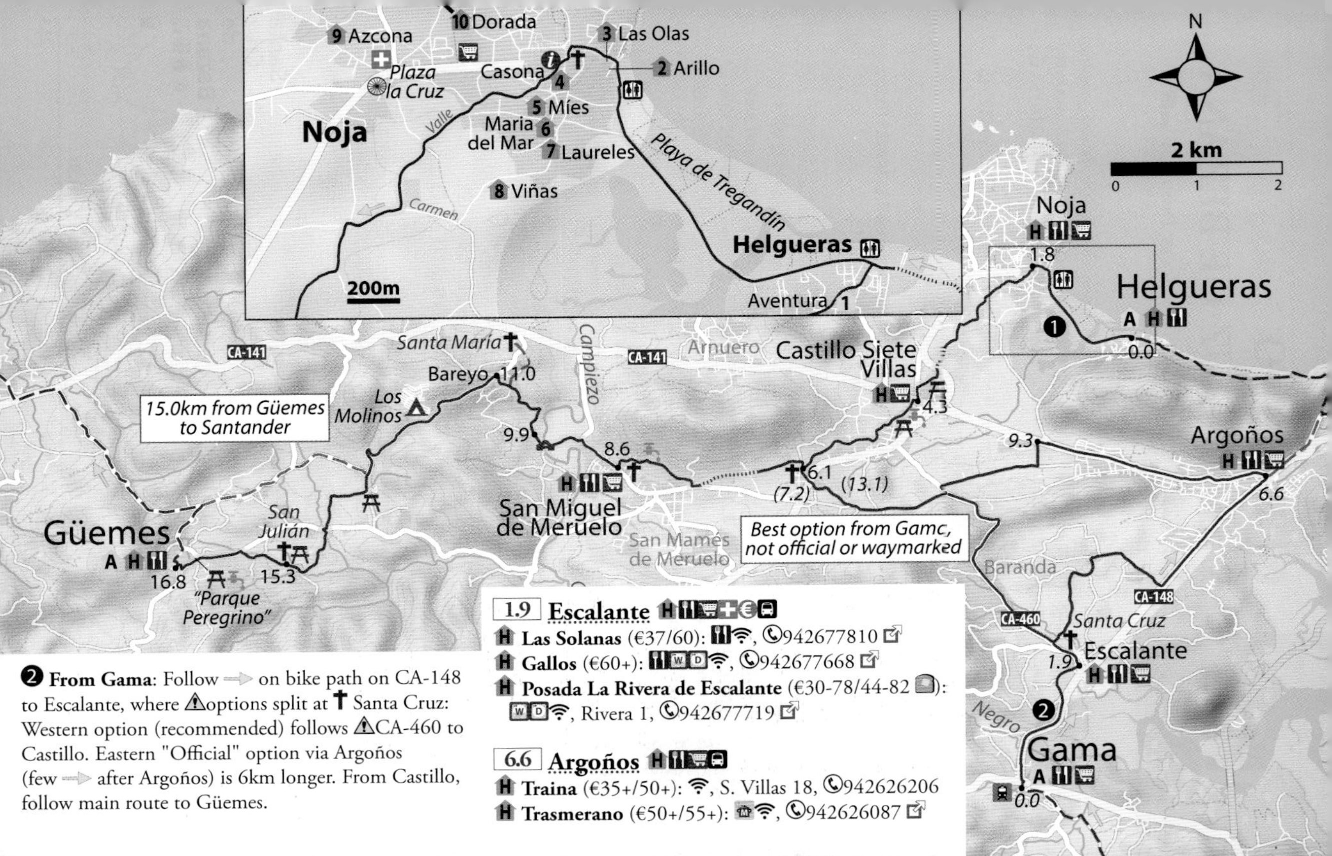

2 From Gama: Follow → on bike path on CA-148 to Escalante, where ⚠options split at ✝ Santa Cruz: Western option (recommended) follows ⚠CA-460 to Castillo. Eastern "Official" option via Argoños (few → after Argoños) is 6km longer. From Castillo, follow main route to Güemes.

1.9 Escalante

- H **Las Solanas** (€37/60): ©942677810
- H **Gallos** (€60+): ©942677668
- H **Posada La Rivera de Escalante** (€30-78/44-82): Rivera 1, ©942677719

6.6 Argoños

- H **Traina** (€35+/50+): S. Villas 18, ©942626206
- H **Trasmerano** (€50+/55+): ©942626087

13 GÜEMES TO SANTA CRUZ DE BEZANA

23.9km (14.9mi), 6.5-8.5 HOURS, DIFFICULTY:

P 69%, 16.6km, U 31%, 7.3km

Enjoy spectacular coastal walking on dirt footpaths along cliffs above the sea, passing splendid beaches. ⚠ Caution on CA-141. Somo-Santander ferry costs €2.85 and leaves every 30 min weekdays, every hour weekends/holidays, Company Los Reginas ✆942216753.

4.4 Galizano: **Vijanera** (€55+): , Canal 1, ✆942505373
Posada el Solar (€40-90): , Barrio Linderrio 56, ✆942505292
La Vijanera (€55+): , La Canal 1, ✆942505373

13.7 Somo: **La Concha** (€40/50): , Cerámica 13, ✆942510325
Las Dunas (€40-60/60-80): , Quebrantas 5, ✆942510040

15.0 Santander All services in this major city.

1. A **Santos Mártires** (asoc, 50, €10-12): , Ruamayor 9, ✆942219747, 3pm (1:30pm summer) all year, very crowded with squeaky beds, no pots and pans
2. A **Hostel Santander** (20, €20-30): , Paseo de Pereda 15, ✆942223986
3. A **Santander Central** (40, €21-26): , Calderón Barca 4, ✆942377540
4. A **Hostel Allegro** (€20-25): , Alta 42, ✆942286649
5. H **Plaza Pombo - La Corza** (€40-60): , Hernán Cortés 25, ✆942212950
6. H **Bahía** (€70-189): , Cádiz 22, ✆902570627
7. H **Plaza** (€32-40/45-64): , Cádiz 13, ✆942212967, near bus/train stations
8. H **Hostal Cabo Mayor** (€55+): , Cádiz 1, ✆942211181
9. H **Pensión Angelines** (€24-30/35-40): , Atilano Rodríguez 9, ✆942312584
10. H **Hospedaje Magellanes** (€29-49/39-69): , Magallanes 22, ✆942371421
11. H **Hostal del Carmen** (€30-40/42-65): , San Fernando 48, ✆942230190
12. H **Art Santander** (€50-150): , Teresa de Jesús 20, ✆942109090
13. H **Le Petit Boutique** (€64+/80+): , Castros 10, ✆942075768

19.9 Peñacastillo
H **San Millán** (€36-57/56-80): , Ortega y Gasset 94, ✆942345677

Continued on map

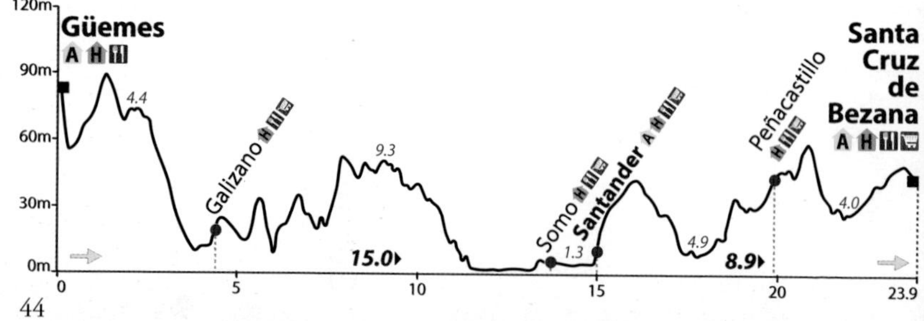

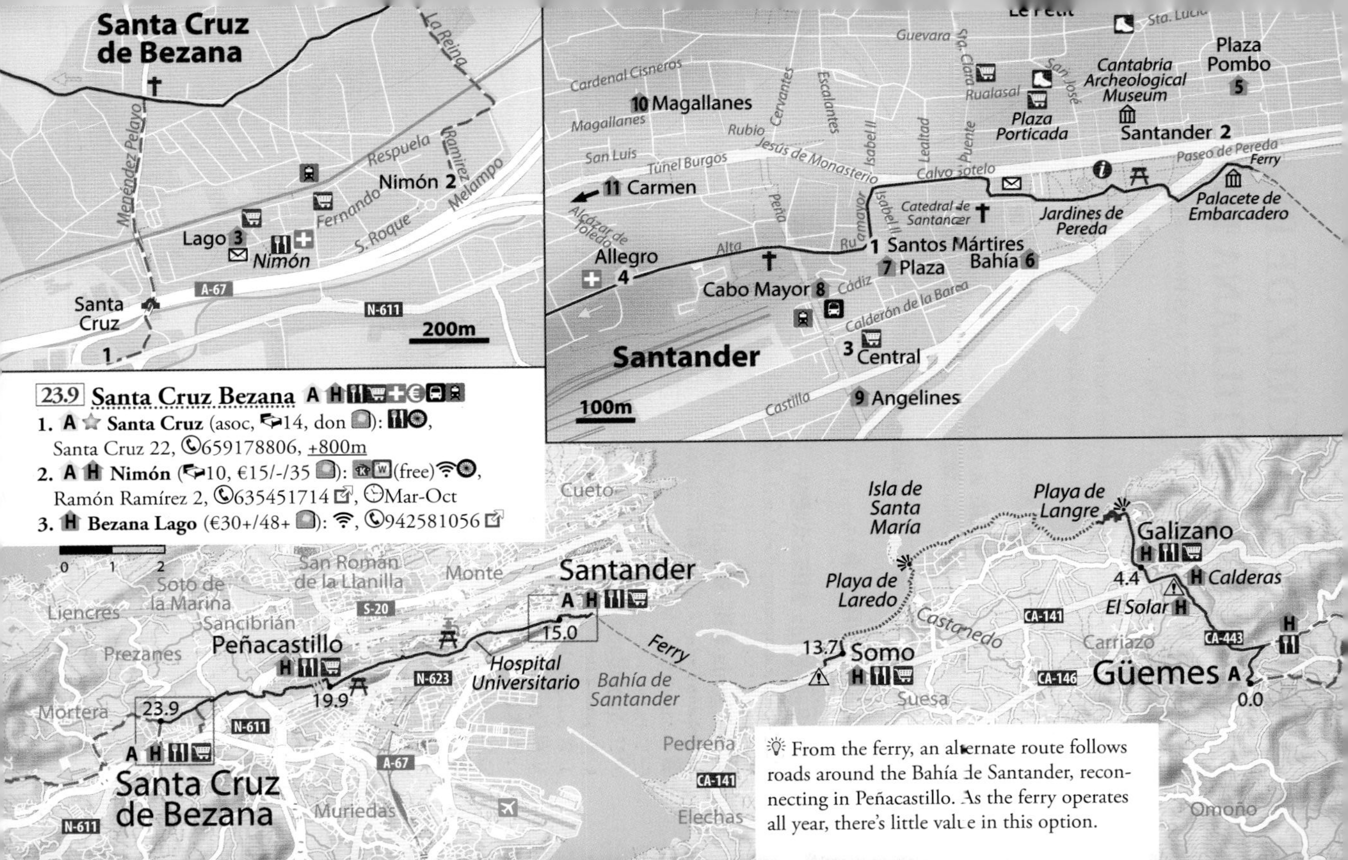

23.9 **Santa Cruz Bezana** A H

1. A ☆ **Santa Cruz** (asoc, 14, don): Santa Cruz 22, 659178806, +800m
2. A H **Nimón** (10, €15/-/35): (free), Ramón Ramírez 2, 635451714, Mar-Oct
3. H **Bezana Lago** (€30+/48+): , 942581056

From the ferry, an alternate route follows roads around the Bahía de Santander, reconnecting in Peñacastillo. As the ferry operates all year, there's little value in this option.

14 SANTA CRUZ DE BEZANA TO SANTILLANA DEL MAR

26.9km (16.7mi), **7.5-9.5 Hours, Difficulty:**
P 87%, 23.4km, U 13%, 3.5km

Take a 2-minute train (€1.65) ride from Boo to Mogro and walk to Santillana del Mar; the long detour adds 8km. ⚠ It's dangerous and illegal to cross the rail bridge on foot.

1.3 Mompía: **Alcamino** (€35/50): , ✆942765976

5.2 Boo Piélagos: **Piedad** (16, €12): , ✆942586115, all year, ⚠ Short train connection between Boo and Mogro.

5.4 Mogro: **Joyuca del Pás** (€50+): , ✆942576647

13.6 Cudón: **Victoria** (€65-95): , Mies Abajo 40, ✆942577723

17.1 Requejada
Clara Campoamor (12, €5): , ✆942082416, all year, keys at Bar Puerto

22.3 Viveda: **Cueli** (€35-50/45-60): , Puente la Barca, ✆942803519
Pensión Lydia (€35-55): , Barrio Pereo 10, ✆942897993
Posada las Tres Mentiras (€28-63/44-68): , Barrio la Pelia 41, ✆942677719

26.9 Santillana del Mar
1. **Jesús Otero** (muni, 16, €6): , ✆942840198, 4pm all year, behind museum
2. **Solar de Hidalgos** (14, €10+/25+/30+): , ✆942818387, all year
3. **Convento** (asoc, 38, €12+): , Antonio Niceas 2, ✆680594138, a. y.
4. **Camping Santillana** (€15+, studio €42+): , ✆942818250
5. **Casa del Marqués** (€70-170): , Cantón 26, ✆942818888
6. **Altamira** (€60/100): , C. 1, ✆942818025
7. **Parador** (€72+): , Ramón Pelayo, ✆942818000
8. **Los Infantes** (€69): , Dor. 1, ✆942818100
9. **Angelica** (€50+): Hornos 3 Pl Mayor, ✆942818238

Continued on map

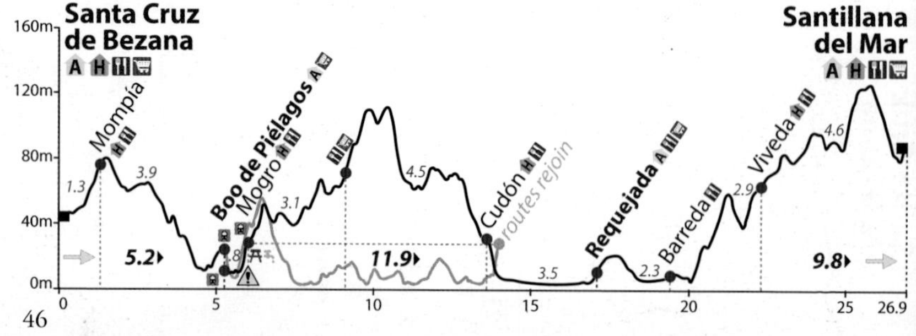

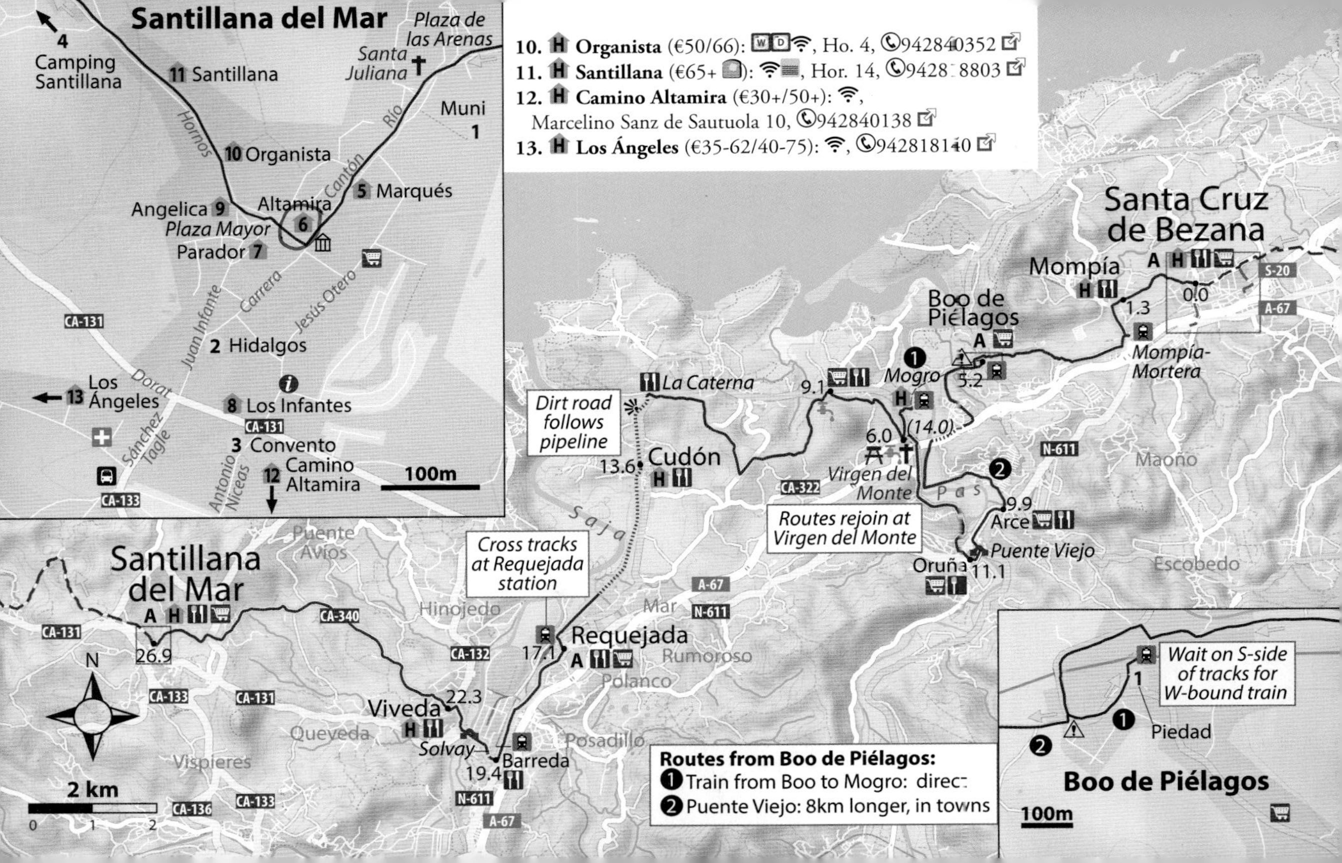
Santillana del Mar
4
Camping Santillana
11 Santillana
10 Organista
Hornos
Plaza de las Arenas
Santa Juliana
Río
Cantón
Muni
1
5 Marqués
Altamira
6
Angelica 9
Plaza Mayor
Parador 7
Carrera
Jesús Otero
Juan Infante
2 Hidalgos
Los Ángeles 13
Dorat
8 Los Infantes
3 Convento
12 Camino Altamira
Sánchez Tagle
Antonio Niceas
CA-131
CA-133
100m
10. Organista (€50/66): Ho. 4, 942840352
11. Santillana (€65+): Hor. 14, 9428_8803
12. Camino Altamira (€30+/50+):
Marcelino Sanz de Sautuola 10, 942840138
13. Los Ángeles (€35-62/40-75): 942818140
Santa Cruz de Bezana
Mompía
S-20
A-67
0.0
1.3
Mompía-Mortera
Boo de Piélagos
5.2
Mogro
(14.0)
9.1
La Caterna
6.0
Virgen del Monte
Dirt road follows pipeline
Cudón
13.6
CA-322
N-611
Maoño
Pas
9.9
Arce
Puente Viejo
Oruña
11.1
Escobedo
Routes rejoin at Virgen del Monte
Saja
Cross tracks at Requejada station
Santillana del Mar
Puente Avíos
Hinojedo
Mar
Requejada
17.1
Rumoroso
Polanco
CA-340
CA-131
CA-132
CA-133
CA-136
26.9
Viveda
22.3
Queveda
Solvay
Barreda
19.4
Posadillo
Vispieres
N
2 km
0 1 2
Routes from Boo de Piélagos:
1 Train from Boo to Mogro: direct
2 Puente Viejo: 8km longer, in towns
Wait on S-side of tracks for W-bound train
Piedad
Boo de Piélagos
100m

15 SANTILLANA DEL MAR TO COMILLAS

22.3km (13.9mi), **6.5-8.5 Hours, Difficulty:**
P 93%, 20.7km, U 7%, 1.6km

3.5 Oreña H: H Oreña (€40-60): , Viallán 262B, 655943983
H Posada La Aldea (€45-55): , Barrio Viallan, 942716091
H Pescador (€45-70): , Barrio Viallán 255, 942716346
H Posada la Roblera (€50-70): , Barrio Viallan 266, 942716104, +300m

6.0 Caborredondo A H
1. **A Izarra** (20, €6): , Barrio Caborredondo 17, 628428167, Mar-Oct
2. **H Posada Cabarredondo** (€55-80): , Barrio Caborredondo 81, 942716181
3. **H Posada San Pedro** (€60+): Barrio San Roque 79, 942716135

11.8 Cóbreces A H
1. **A Abadía Cisterciense Viaceli** (par, 24, €6): , Corrales 191, 942725017, vespers
2. **A El Pino** (12, €15-20): , Pino 1, 620437962, 12pm Apr-Oct
3. **A H Viejo Lucas** (134, €14/20/34): , Pino 43, 625483596, a. y.
4. **H Posada Las Mañanitas** (€40/50+): , Antoñán 88, 942725238
5. **H Pensión Bella Vista** (€30/40): , Playa 240, 942725221
6. **H Sanmar** (€40-65/55-85): , Playa de Luaña, 942725305

18.0 La Iglesia/Ruiloba H A
H A Camping Helguero (bungalow €65+, A€13): , 942722124

22.3 Comillas A H
1. **A La Peña** (muni, 20, €6): , La Peña, 942720033, 4pm Apr-Oct
2. **H Hostal Esmeralda** (€40-60/60-80): , Antonio López 7, 942720097
3. **H Pensión Villa** (€25-55): , Antonio López 22, 665309088
4. **H Mar** (€50-85/65-110): , Paseo del Jarón, 942722499
5. **H Pensión La Aldea II** (€40-60): Campios 18, 942721046
6. **H Pasaje San Jorge** (€45+/65+): C. D. Campa 14, 942720915
7. **H Solana Montañesa** (€60-85): , La Campa 22, 942720915

Continued on map

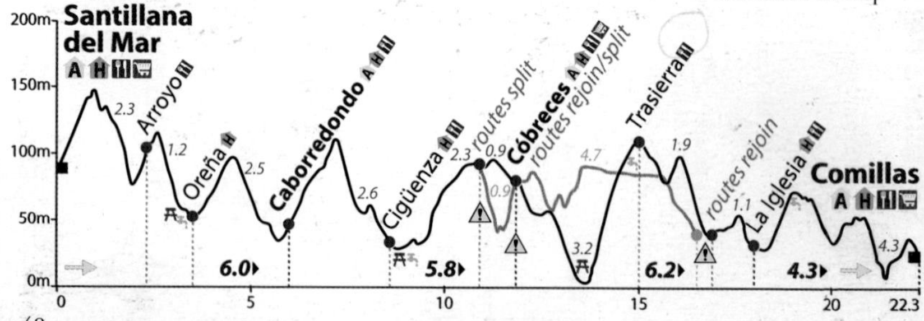

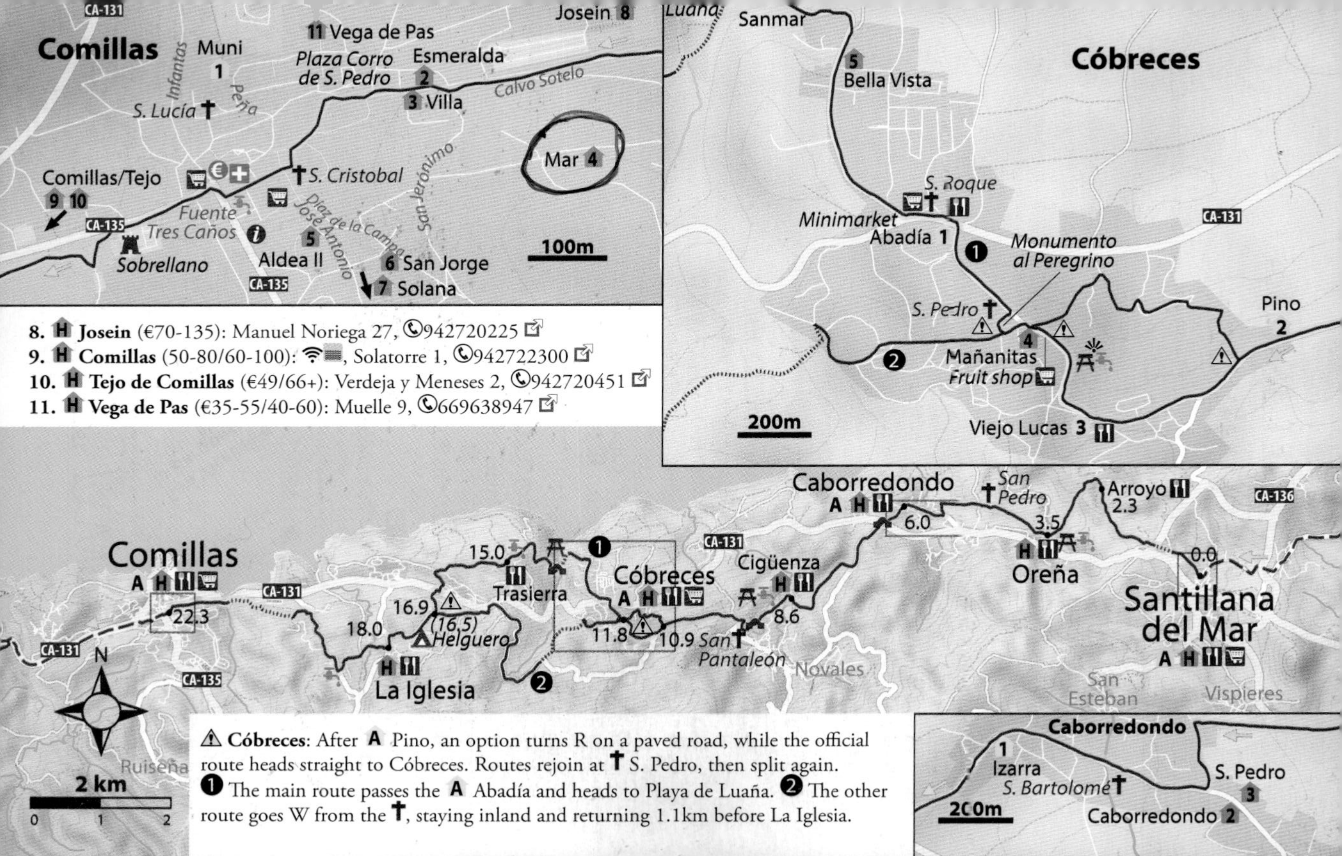

8. Josein (€70-135): Manuel Noriega 27, 942720225
9. Comillas (50-80/60-100): Solatorre 1, 942722300
10. Tejo de Comillas (€49/66+): Verdeja y Meneses 2, 942720451
11. Vega de Pas (€35-55/40-60): Muelle 9, 669638947

⚠ **Cóbreces**: After A Pino, an option turns R on a paved road, while the official route heads straight to Cóbreces. Routes rejoin at ✝ S. Pedro, then split again. ❶ The main route passes the A Abadía and heads to Playa de Luaña. ❷ The other route goes W from the ✝, staying inland and returning 1.1km before La Iglesia.

16

COMILLAS TO COLOMBRES

28.9km (18.0mi), **8-10.5 Hours, Difficulty:**

P 92%, 26.7km, U 8%, 2.2km

The route splits after crossing the Capitán River: ❶ The recommended, official route continues straight on a paved multi-use path and generally along the coast, ➡ are few, but navigation easy. ❷ Ascends left on a paved road; initial ➡ is gone, then marks are visible.

Oyambre Natural Park

4.8 **Oyambre** H A: H **Sofia** (€60-82): Oyambre 26C, 942091231

6.6 H **Gerra Mayor** (€40+/50+): 609096630, +500m

H **Pensión Oyambre** (€20-41): Gerra 6, 942746082

(5.4) **Posada El Teju** (€30-50): Barrio la Cara El Tejo 942709639, on ❷

(8.0) **Revilla** A, on ❷ alternate route

A **Aventura** (24, €10): 942712075, all year, +600m

A **Surf Gerra** (21, €15): 627944523, Easter-Oct, +2km

11.3 San Vicente de la Barquera

1. H **Arenal** (€27/40+): Arenal 17, 942710225, key at Confeitaria Carma
2. H **Luzón** (€30-45/50-70): Miramar 1, 942710050
3. H **El Corro** (€25-45): Antonio del Corro 1, 942712613
4. H **Azul de Galimar** (€50-95/60-115): Cam. de Santiago 11, 942715020
5. H **Alto Santiago** (€42-65): Calzadas 9, 942710121
6. H **Las Calzadas** (€35-50/45-100): Calzadas 16, 609418831

19.3 Serdio A H

1. A **Municipal** (16, €5): 664108003, all year, if closed ask for Kety
2. H **Posada La Torre** (€70): Aldea 2, 942718462
3. H **Hosteria El Corralucu** (€45-55): El Corralucu 15, 942718566
4. H **Fuente de las Anjanas** (€27/54): Canal de los Bueyes, 942718539

22.4 Muñorrodero H

H **Posada de Muño** (€40-60): Muñorrodero 8, 942718058

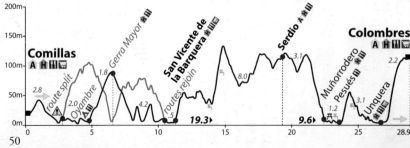

Continued on map

200m
150m
100m
50m
0m
Comillas A H
route split
2.8
2.0
Oyambre A
1.8
Gerra Mayor H
4.2
San Vicente de la Barquera H
routes rejoin
.5
19.3
8.0
Serdio A H
3.1
9.6
Muñorrodero H
Pesués
1.2
3.1
Unquera H
2.2
Colombres A H
0 5 10 15 20 25 28.9

Unquera

H **Canal** (€27/43): wifi, P. Estación, ☎942717101

H **Hostal Río Deva** (€25-35/35-45): wifi, San Felipe Neri 10, ☎942717157

H **El Rincón de Bustio** (€90-115): wifi, Capilla, ☎985412525

28.9 Colombres A H

A H **El Cantu** (120, €12/20/40): wifi, ☎985412075, Mar-Oct, adventure & beach sports, often full of youth groups in summer, distinctive bright blue building

H **Villa Manola** (apt 2pax €65, 4pax €100): Redondo, ☎985412068

H **Casa Junco** (€35/55): wifi, Peral, ☎985412243, 1.4km after town

H **Oyambre** (€15 per person): Peral 11, ☎985412242, 1.4km after town

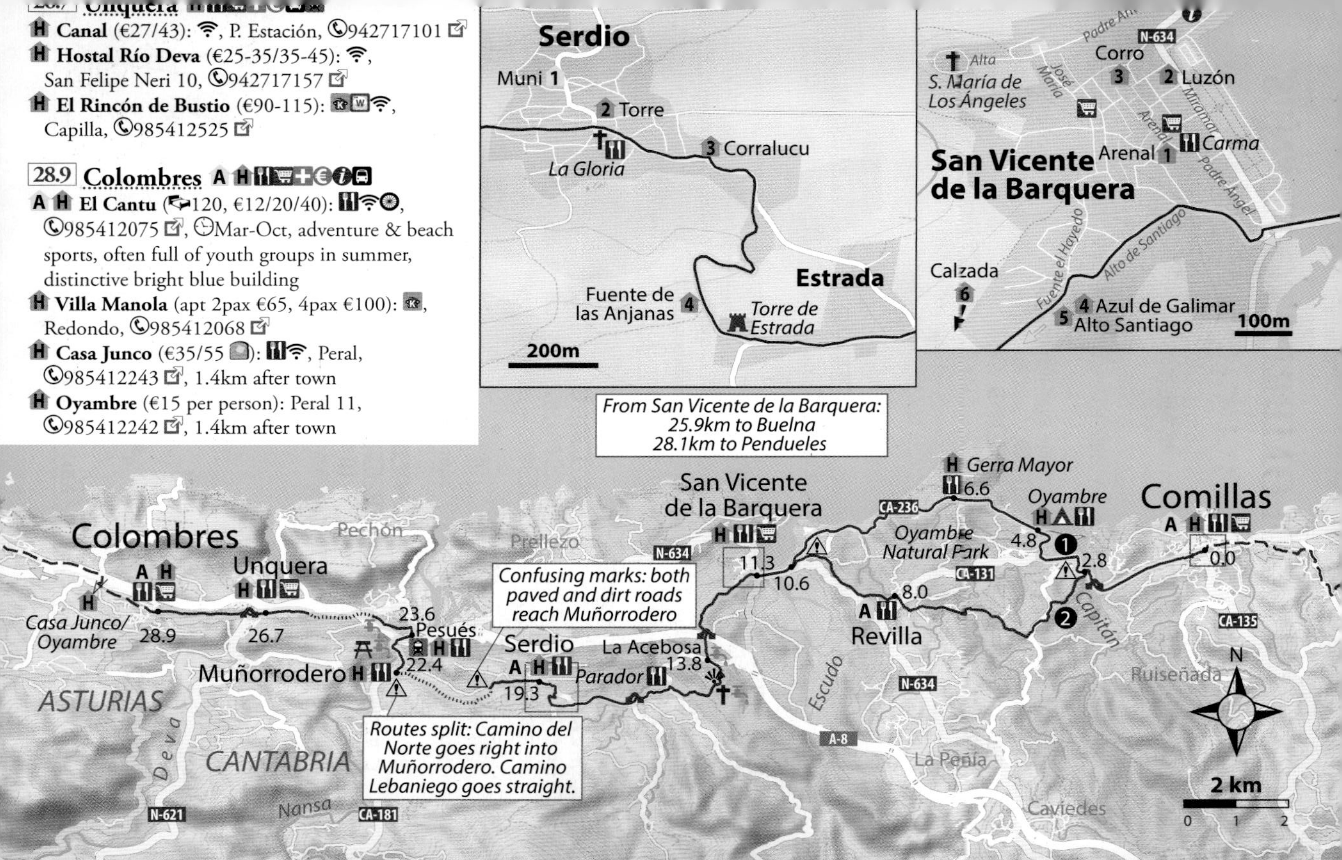

17 COLOMBRES TO LLANES

25.4km (15.8mi), 7.5-9.5 HOURS, DIFFICULTY:
28%, 7.0km, 72%, 18.4km

Soak in the best views of the entire route. Gaze up at the Picos de Europa to the South!

3.2 La Franca
Route splits after town.

A **Triskel** (12, €15): Corral Abajo 50A, 667206617, Feb-Nov
A H **Renacer** (10, €15/-/40): 678169939, all year
A H **Playa de la Franca** (cabin €15/person, dbl €65): 985412222
H **Pensión La Casa Abajo** (€35): Ctra N-634 km 285, 985412430
H **La Parra** (€25-35/40-50): Ctra N-634 km 285, 985412234

8.2 Buelna

1. A H **S. Marina** (60, €10/-/45+): 985411218, Easter-Oct
2. H **Casa Rural de Aldea El Valle** (€40-55): El Valle, 985411187/615543591

10.7 Pendueles
From Pendueles, follow the E-9 walking route to Llanes.

1. A **Aves de Paso** (14, don): 645561638, Apr-Sept closed Fridays
2. A H **Casa Flor** (15, €8-12/-/40): El Rubino, 680663472, Apr-Oct
3. H **Bar Castiellu** (€25/30): La Quintana, 985411390
4. H **La Casa en el Camino** (€72/80): Barrio de Verines 97, 610273109

13.6 Vidiago

A **Caserón Vidiago** (18, €10): N-634, 985404446, Mar-Oct, +750m
H **La Casona de Vidiago** (€48-86): Barrio del Cueto, 985411069
H **Bufón de Arenillas** (€63-83): Riegu, 985411345

19.2 Andrín
H **Casona de Andrín** (€70-80): Andrín, 985417250
H **La Boriza** (€60-80/75-100): Camino de la Playa, 985417049

25.4 Llanes

1. A **Estación** (40, €15+): Estación Feve, 985401458, Mar-Nov
2. A H **Casona** (44, €15/35/50): Encarnación 3, 985402494
3. A **Juvenîl** (82, €12): Celso Amieva 7, 984106660, all year, poor reviews

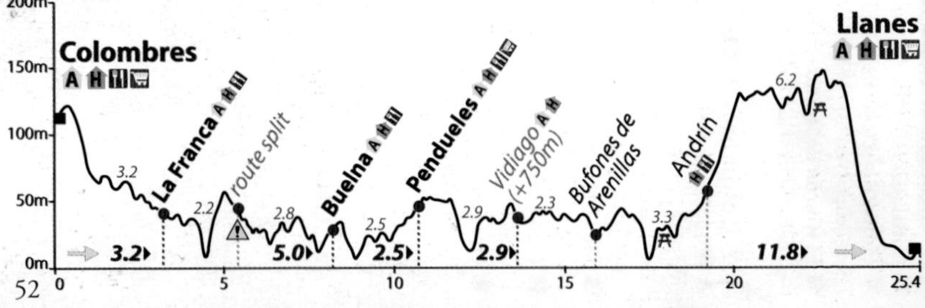

4. Senda del Peregrino

5. A H **Portilla** (48, €15-20/-/80): 985401466, May-Sept, at H Alonso

6. H **Gran Hotel Paraiso** (€175+): Pidal 2, 985402325

7. H **Las Rocas** (€50/60+): Marqués de Canillejas 3, 985402431

8. H **Los Molinos** (€55-100): Cotiello Bajo 7 985400707

9. H **Posada Rey** (€50+): Mayor 11, 985401332

10. H **Iberia** (€30+): Castillo 4, 627891676

11. H **Don Paco** (€60+): Encarnacion 1, 985400150

12. H **Sablon** (€50+): Moría 1, 985400787

13. H **Los Pinos** (€45+): 985401116, +400m

14. H **La Palma** (€50/62+): 985401726

After La Franca, the route splits:
❶ Better option is an unofficial, route that crosses N-634 and railroad tracks to footpaths near the sea. This route cuts back to Buelna, passing the hidden Playa de Cobijeru before heading back to the sea on the way to Pendueles. ❷ Official route follows N-634 to Buelna and Pendueles.

18 LLANES TO CUERRES

23.4km (14.5mi), **6.5-8 Hours, Difficulty:**
P 63%, 14.7km, U 37%, 8.7km

A pleasant day passing through several coastal villages; Ribadesello is an additional 6.7km.

2.7 **Poó** A H Pronounced "Po." A H Llanes Playa oriented toward surfers.

1. A **Cambarina** (16, €12-15): , Higos 128, 635739837, Mar-Oct
2. A H **Llanes Playa** (25, €12+/-/30+): , 985403181, +300m
3. H **El Camín** (€55-80/60-120): , Paseo de Llanes, 985402301
4. H **Villa Miramar** (€60/70+): Barrio de los Higos, 985401460
5. H **Cuartamenteru** (€41-81): , Barrio Anteji, 985403276
6. H **Farola** (€55-90): , Playa de Poó, 985401250

5.5 **Celorio** A H Touristy coastal town.

1. A **Palmeras** (20, €12.50+): , Abajo 120, 638287065, Mar-Oct, not available in summer
2. H **Gavitu** (€40-50/65-80): Barrio Gavitu, 985400588, +700m

7.3 **Barro** H: H **Miracielos** (€45/65+): , Cabila 373, 699976921
H **Hostal la Playa** (€50-70): Ctra de la Playa, 985400766

13.5 **Naves** H: H **Hotel La Fonte** (€35/50+): , Plaza Santa Ana, 985408696
H **Villa Marrón** (€40-80/50-94): , Ctra AS-263, 985407372

14.5 **Villahormes** A H
A H **Camino Santiago Villahormes** (24, €10+/-/35+): , 639418767
H **Apartamentos Rurales La Canalina** (€50-115): , 619180870, +500m

17.8 **Nueva** H Last until Ribadeo.

1. H **San Jorge** (€35-50/45-65): Tilos 96, 985410285
2. H **Cuevas del Mar** (€55-80): , Pl. de Laverde Ruiz, 985410377
3. H **Luna del Valle** (€28/38+): , Barrio La Nogalera, 985410713
4. H **Casa de Indianos San Tomás** (€60): , Plaza del Hospital, 985410039

Continued on map

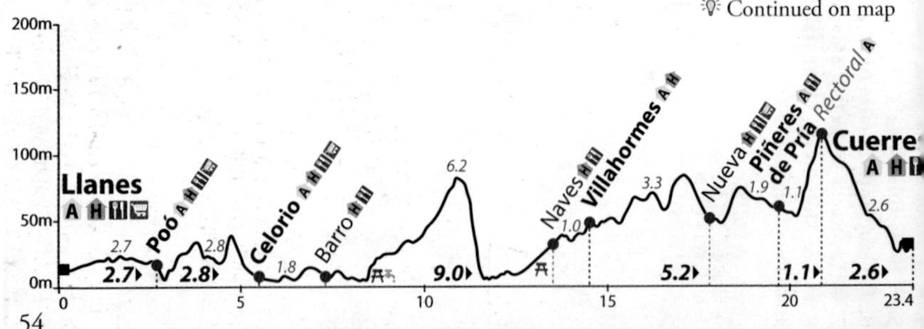

19.7 **Piñeres de Pría** A H Basic supplies at Casa Rectoral, 1.1km after Piñeres

A **La Llosa de Cosme** (10, €10): P. Pría 16, 609861373, all year

A **Casa Rectoral** (54, €6): 617942141, Jun-Aug, far from services

H **Hotel Rural Alfoz** (€35/50+): Barrio Rondiella 9, 985410495

23.4 **Cuerres** A H Train station called Belmonte.

1. A **Belén** (6, don): Cuerres 25F, 634443755, 2pm all year, **closed, reopening unknown**
2. A H **Reposo Andayón** (10, don/-/€60): Barr. Güera, 639677933
3. H **Villalén** (€40/50): 985857093, +300m
4. H **Hotel Rural Aldea del Trasgu** (€50-75/65-85): 985861504

19 CUERRES TO LA ISLA

22.8km (14.2mi), **6.5-8.5 Hours, Difficulty:**
P 63%, 14.3km, U 37%, 8.5km

The route passes secluded beaches on the way to La Isla. On the W edge of Playa Arenal de Morís, the route joins a paved road and continues briefly inland before following dirt paths back along the coast. It's possible to skip the paved road entirely and continue on dirt paths closer to the coast before rejoining the official route ahead.

6.7 **Ribadesella** A H Day's largest town; good place to resupply.
1. A H **Sauces** (8, €5-15/45/65): , 985861312, 2.6km past town
2. A H **Alojamiento Santa Ana** (pilgrim rate €17-20): Sella 2, 615545743
3. A H **Ribadesella** (€17/-/34): , Manuel Caso d/Villa 38 5A, 642762155
4. H **Arbidel** (€30-40/40-70): , Oscura 1, 985860633
5. H **Marina** (€35/55+): , Gran Vía 36, 985860050
6. H **Argüelles** (€40-70): , del Sol 9, 985861810
7. H **Apartamentos Las Vegas** (€55/70+): , Atalaya, 606334556
8. H **Villa Rosario** (€57-130): , Dionisio Ruisánchez 6, 985860090
9. H **Don Pepe Ría** (€65-75): , Dionisio Ruisánchez 15, 985857881

11.3 **San Esteban de Leces** A **Municipal** (38, €6): , 985857611, 4pm all year, nearest restaurant 1.5km by bus, or bar de Berbes may deliver 638420629

13.2 **La Vega** A H Route from La Vega is scenic, follows narrow, rocky footpaths.
1. A **Tu Casa** (7, don): , La Sertal 21, 984100746, Mar-Oct, closed Fridays
2. H **Casa L'Arcu** (€40-45): del Sol 4, 691340424
3. H **Playa de Vega** (€60-85): , Finca El Cuetu, 985858084

22.8 **La Isla** A H Most services and A (register at Angelita's) are off route.
1. ⚠ A **Municipal**: , Castro 85, 985852005, **closed 2018, unknown reopening**
2. A **Furacu** (y. h., 40, €20): , M. E. Hidalgo 196, 985856661, Jun-Aug
3. H **The Island** (€70-100): , Francisco Carrillo, 985856115 +600m
4. H **La Isla** (€30-60/40-80): , Francisco Carrillo, 985856001
5. H **Monte y Mar** (€29+/38+): , Crta de la Isla 306, 985856561
6. H **Los Caspios** (€55-130): , Crta de la Isla, 985852098

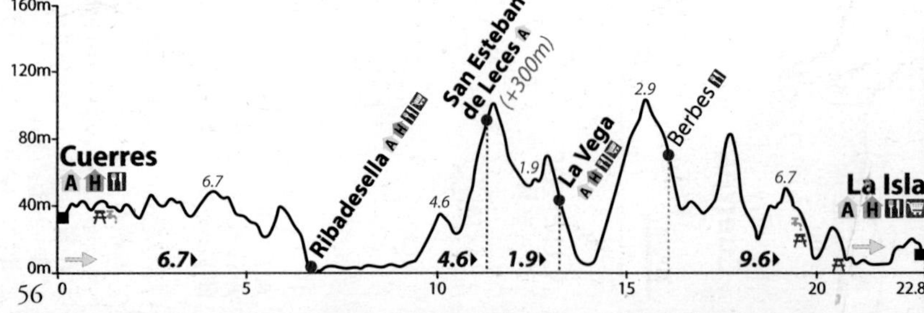

La Isla
Playa de la Espasa
Playa de Moracey
Playa de la Beciella
Playa Arenal de Morís
22.8
A-8
Gobiendes
Espasa
Lloroñi
N-632
Arenal de Morís
16.1
Berbes
Be careful walking along highway (N-632)
La Vega
13.2
11.3
S. Esteban de Leces, +300m
9.3
Sauces
Ribadesella
6.7
Cuerres
0.0
AS-263
Collera
Meluerda
Camango
Llovio
Sella
Omedina
Santianes
Fries
N-634
El Llano
Riensena
2 km
0
1
2
N
La Vega
Vega
Path can be very muddy when wet
200m
1 Tu Casa
2 L'Arcu
3 Playa de Vega
Pepe 9
8 Rosario
Parque Malecón
walking path along river
3 Ribadesella
2 Santa Ana
7 Las Vegas
6 Argüelles
1 Sauces (2.6km)
5 Marina
4 Arbidel
Ribadesella
200m
La Isla
Municipal 1
Angelita's House
Island 3
La Isla 4
5 Monte y Mar
2 Furacu
6 Caspios
Bueño
200m

20

LA ISLA TO VILLAVICIOSA

21.5km (13.4mi), 6.5-8 HOURS, DIFFICULTY:
P 74%, 16.0km, U 26%, 5.5km

Head inland through forested hills and charming villages to Villaviciosa, famous for its cider.

3.7 **Colunga** Few services until Villaviciosa; vending machines enroute.
1. **Mar del Sueve** (€56-86/70-108): Asturias 22, 985852111
2. **Fitu** (€30/35+): Asturias 35, 672356442
3. **Las Vegas** (€28-35/35-55): Asturias 11, 985856025
4. **Villa de Colunga** (€27-30/40-50): Playa 10, 984841196
5. **Entreviñes** (€48-67): Entreviñes, 985852631, +500m
6. **El Sueve** (€45): Solrivero, 985856266, on route 500m past center

9.1 **Pernús** **La Casona de Fraile** (€30-36/35-42): 985856492

12.2 **Priesca** A H No but A sells basic supplies
A H **Rectoral** (22, €12/-/24): Quintana 2, 636056520, a. y.

15.2 **Sebrayo** A **Municipal** (14, €4): Sebrayo 21, 699440399, Mar-Oct, food truck comes in afternoon, water may not be potable, key in house #7 (L turn 50m past A)

18.1 **Muslera** A **La Llamarga** (8, don): 985892501, Mar-Oct

21.5 **Villaviciosa** A H Stock up on food—next grocery in Gijón.
1. A **Villaviciosa** (28, €13+): Marqués V. 5, 607326927, all year
2. A **Congreso** (32, €10-15/-/25-42): Ay. 25, 660615660, Mar-Nov
3. A **La Payariega** (10, don): Payariega 7, 651068840, 1.5km before
4. H **Carlos I** (€45/60+): Plaza Carlos I, 985890121
5. H **Casa España** (€35/40+): Plaza Carlos I 3, 985892030
6. H **Murias Blancas** (€59-75): V. G. Concha 12, 985893366
7. H **Avenida Real** (€45/70): Carmen 10, 985892047
8. H **El Conventín** (€37+): El Carmen 14, 985893389
9. H **Manquín** (€40-60/50-70): S. Clara 2, 985890024

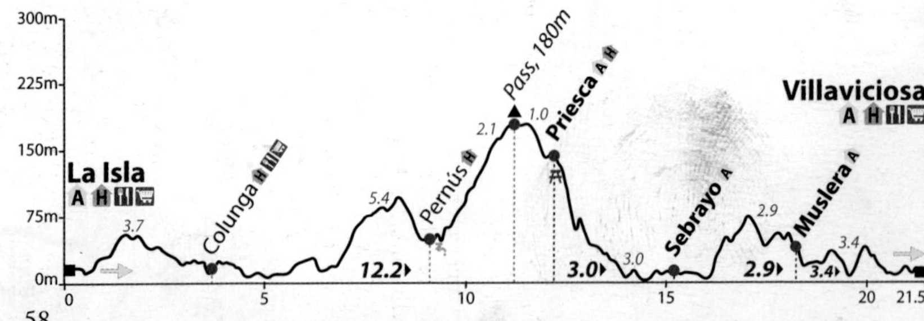

Muslera
+600m
Sebrayo
Castiello de Lué
San Telmo
Colunga
Güerres
La Isla
16.5
18.1
15.2
Peregrín Cansau (vending machine)
20.0
La Payariega, +200m
12.2
Pass, 180m
Priesca
La Llera
El Lovéu
Pernús
La Vega
9.1
Conyéu
Beldredo
La Riera
3.7
0.0
21.5
Villaviciosa
Amandí
Gobiendes
Lloroñi
Espasa
Lue
Sales
Selorio
Highly recommended
A ☆ Ferrería is just 2.4km further in Amandí.
In Colunga and Villaviciosa, most hotels offer a special €20/person rate for pilgrims (minimum two persons, subject to availability), called the "Cider Shire Pilgrim Pass."
Villaviciosa
Pando Valle
Alejandro Casona
Víctor García de la Concha
Magdalena
Marqués
Cavanillas
N. Rivero
Balbín Busto
Carmen
6 Murias Blancas
3 Payariega (1.5km)
Carlos I
Villaviciosa
España 5
4
1
2 Congreso
7 Avenida Real
8 Conventín
9 Manquín
100m
Colunga
Entreviñes 5
Villa de Colunga 4
Las Vegas 3
2 Fitu
1
Mar del Sueve
6 Sueve
Right onto CL-1 toward Perús
Liberdón
100m
2 km
0
1
2
N

21

VILLAVICIOSA TO GIJÓN

29.9km (18.6mi), **9-11 Hours, Difficulty:**
P 76%, 22.6km, U 24%, 7.3km

After several flatter days, the walk to Gijón includes two significant ascents and 900m total elevation gain. The climbing comes with pleasant walking through forested terrain and wonderful views. ⚠ Shortly after Amandí, there is an option to turn off to the L to Oviedo to join the Camino Primitivo or return to the Norte route in Avilés (see our Camino Primitivo map guide).

2.4 Amandí A H A

Few services from Amandí (2.4km) to Camping Deva (22.1km).

1. **A A Ferrería** (12, don): , Ferrería 1, 646516846, Mar-Oct
2. **H Casona de Amandí** (€77-100/99-125): , San Juan de Amandi 6, 985893411

22.1 Deva A A

A A Camping Deva (36, €6): , Pasadiella 85, 985133848, all year, wooden cabins/4 beds, feels like summer camp, bus to Gijón available (7.5km)

29.9 Gijón A H , A

Peregrin 3.2km before city center

1. **A H Cimadevilla** (shared rooms, 23, €15): , Plaza de la Colegiata, 984198504, student housing available to pilgrims in summer
2. **A Peregrin** (28, €12-15): , P. Pimentel 251, 637993443, a. y., mixed reviews
3. **H Don Pelayo** (€30-60): , San Bernardo 22, 985344450
4. **H Hospedaje Covadonga** (€28-48/35-65): , Libertad 10, 985341685
5. **H Pensión Avilesina** (€20/30): , Corrida 38, 985342939, mixed reviews
6. **H Castilla** (€35-60/40-80): , Corrida 50, 985346200
7. **H Hernán Cortés** (€50-126): , Fernández Vallín 5, 985346000
8. **H Playa Poniente** (€40+): , Marqués de San Esteban 49, 985346063
9. **H Avenida** (€31/37+): , Robustiana Armiño 4, 985352843
10. **H Pensión Plaza** (€30-55/40-70): , Decano Prendes Pando 2, 985346562
11. **H San Miguel** (€38-75/45-84): , Marqués de Casa Valdés 8, 985340025
12. **H Hostal Campoamor** (€28-48/35-65): , Costa 8, 985344939
13. **H Parador** (€75-160): , Torcuato F. Miranda 15, 985370511, 15% p.d.
14. **H Arena** (€59-87/70-120): , Dr. Aquilino Hurlé 31, 985339700
15. **H Polar** (€39/42+): , Juan Carlos I 20, 984296403, 10% pilgrim discount

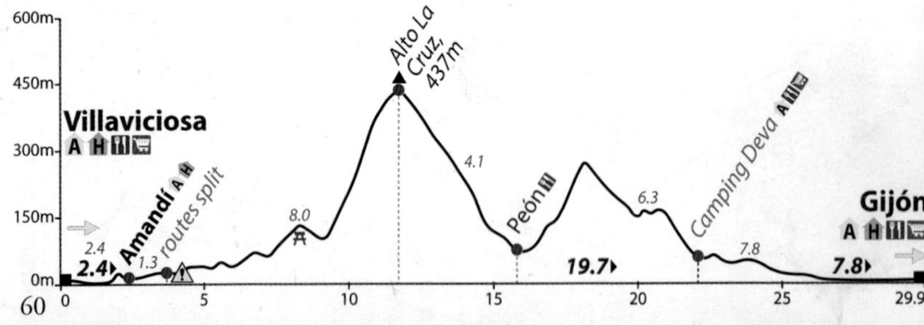

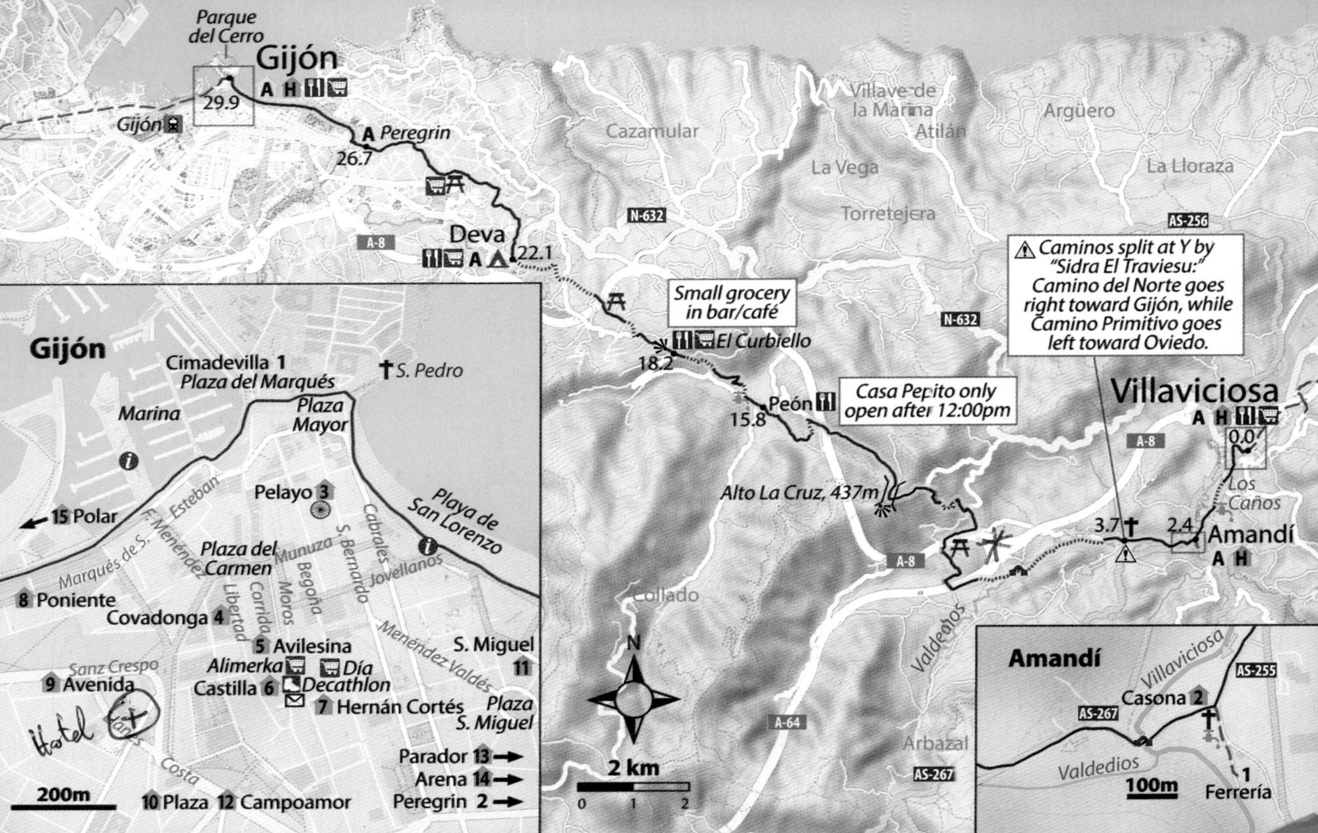

Parque del Cerro
Gijón
29.9
Gijón
A Peregrin
26.7
Deva
22.1
A-8
Cazamular
Villave de la Marina
Atilán
Argüero
La Vega
La Lloraza
Torretejera
N-632
AS-256
Small grocery in bar/café
El Curbiello
18.2
Peón
15.8
Casa Pepito only open after 12:00pm
Caminos split at Y by "Sidra El Traviesu:" Camino del Norte goes right toward Gijón, while Camino Primitivo goes left toward Oviedo.
Villaviciosa
0.0
Los Caños
3.7
2.4
Amandí
Alto La Cruz, 437m
Collado
Valdeaños
A-64
Arbazal
AS-267
N
2 km
0
1
2
Gijón
Cimadevilla 1
Plaza del Marqués
S. Pedro
Marina
Plaza Mayor
Pelayo 3
Playa de San Lorenzo
15 Polar
Marqués de S. Esteban
F. Menéndez
Plaza del Carmen
Munuza
S. Bernardo
Cabrales
Jovellanos
Libertad
Corrida
Moros
Begoña
8 Poniente
Covadonga 4
5 Avilesina
Alimerka
Día
Castilla 6
Decathlon
7 Hernán Cortés
Menéndez Valdés
S. Miguel
11
Plaza S. Miguel
Sanz Crespo
9 Avenida
Costa
200m
10 Plaza
12 Campoamor
Parador 13
Arena 14
Peregrin 2
Amandí
Villaviciosa
AS-255
Casona 2
AS-267
Valdedios
100m
1
Ferrería

22 GIJÓN TO AVILÉS

25.3km (15.7mi), 7-8.5 HOURS, DIFFICULTY:
P 81%, 20.6km, U 19%, 4.7km

This day provides a number of enjoyable kilometers of walking through sparely-populated hills before Tamón, and the last few kilometers on a paved pedestrian way along the Avilés River are decent. However, the section between Tamón and the pedestrian way is quite a slog through industrial areas and along highway AS-19. This is the most unpleasant section of the Camino del Norte. The day can easily be skipped by train from Gijón to Avilés if you desire. In Avilés, the Camino route from Oviedo rejoins 20m before the A municipal albergue.

Consider walking an additional 7.5km to San Martín de Laspra to the wonderful albergue A San Martín to leave a manageable 31.4km to Soto de Luiña the following day.

20.3 Trasona

H **Terra Mar** (€15/25): , Silvota 4, 984119875
H **A Feira Posada** (€50/60): , Overo, 985578664, +1km

25.3 Avilés

1. A **Pedro Solís** (muni, 56, €6): , Gutierrez Herrero 1, 984703117, 1pm (4pm in low season), all year
2. H **Puente Azud** (€25/35-40): , Acero 5, 985550177
3. H **NH Collection Palacio de Avilés** (€67+): , Plaza España 9, 985129080
4. H **Palacio Valdés** (€54-108): , Llano Ponte 4, 984112111
5. H **40 Nudos** (€50-85): , La Fruta 9, 985525754
6. H **Pensión La Fruta** (€35/45+): , La Fruta 19, 985566132
7. H **Don Pedro** (€50/60+): , La Fruta 22, 985512288
8. H **Villalegre** (€36-63/40-71): , Santa Apolonia 60, 985572728

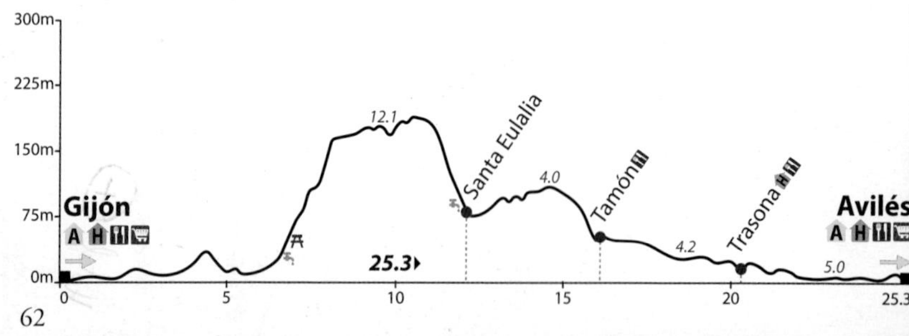

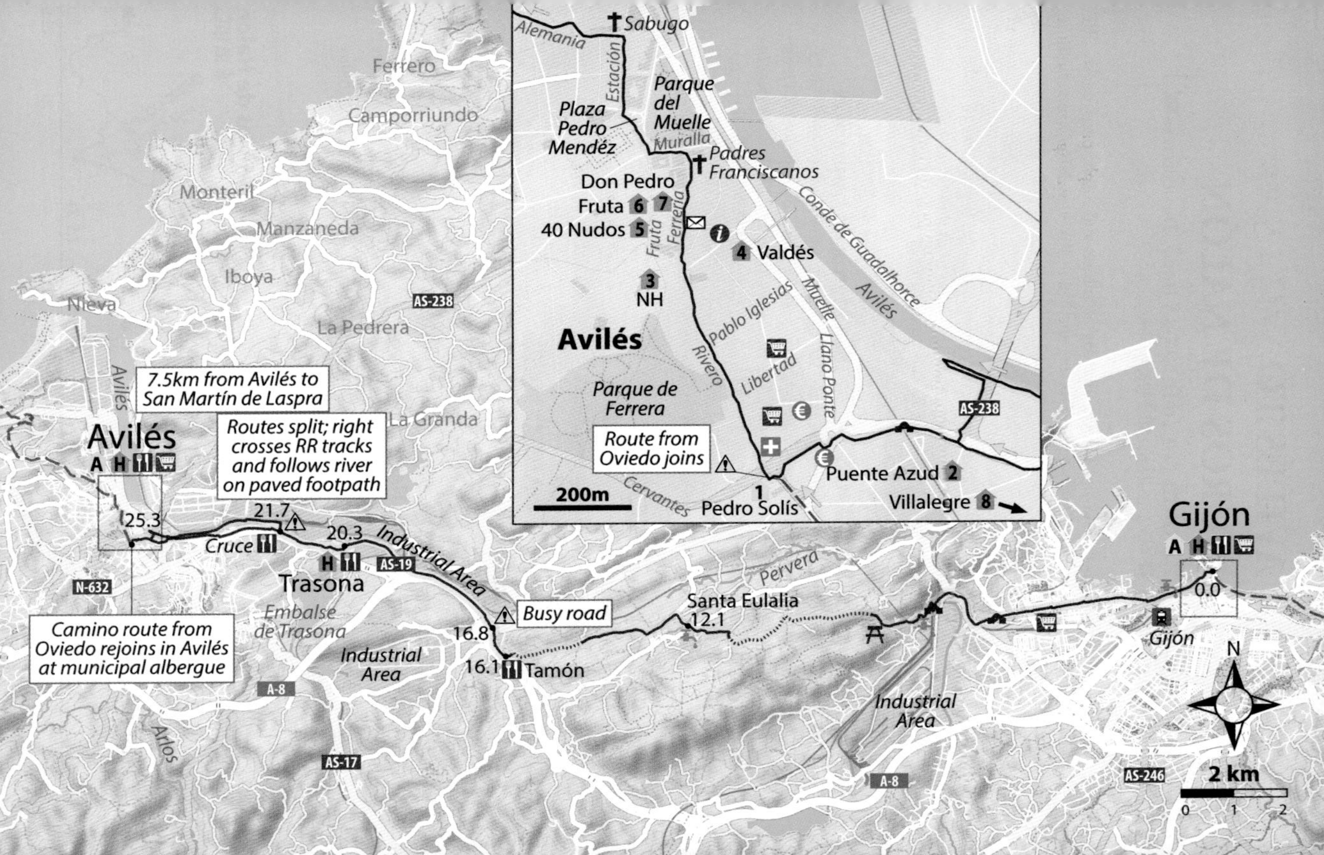

Avilés
A H
7.5km from Avilés to San Martín de Laspra
Routes split; right crosses RR tracks and follows river on paved footpath
Camino route from Oviedo rejoins in Avilés at municipal albergue
25.3
21.7
Cruce
20.3
Trasona
H
Industrial Area
Busy road
16.8
16.1
Tamón
Santa Eulalia
12.1
Pervera
Embalse de Trasona
Industrial Area
Industrial Area
Gijón
A H
0.0
Gijón
N
2 km
0
1
2
Ferrero
Camporriundo
Monteril
Manzaneda
Iboya
Nieva
La Pedrera
La Granda
Avilés
Arlos
AS-238
N-632
AS-19
A-8
AS-17
A-8
AS-246
Sabugo
Alemania
Estación
Plaza Pedro Mendéz
Parque del Muelle
Muralla
Padres Franciscanos
Don Pedro
Fruta 6 7
40 Nudos 5
Fruta
Ferrería
4 Valdés
3
NH
Conde de Guadalhorce
Avilés
Avilés
Pablo Iglesias
Muelle
Llano Ponte
Rivero
Libertad
Parque de Ferrera
AS-238
Route from Oviedo joins
Puente Azud 2
200m
Cervantes
1
Pedro Solís
Villalegre 8

23 AVILÉS TO MUROS DE NALÓN

22.8km (14.2mi), 7-8.5 HOURS, DIFFICULTY:
P 71%, 16.1km, U 29%, 6.7km

Leave industrial areas behind and enjoy a nice day of villages and forested dirt tracks. The route winds south to Soto del Barco before crossing the Nalón River on N-632 and climbing to Muros de Nalón.

Some signage along the way suggests walking from Avilés to Soto de Luiña in one day—quite a task given the distance (35.3km) and significant elevation change. If you'd like to make it to Cadavedo in two days from Avilés, walk past Muros de Nalón to El Pito (extra 4.9km), leaving 30.4km to Cadavedo the following day. If you choose to go to El Pito, be aware that the last grocery store before Soto de Luiña is in Muros de Nalón.

6.3 Salinas A H / 7.5 San Martín de Laspra A

1. A H San Martín (46, don): Barrio Navalón 39, 659803290, 1pm all year, communal meals or will help obtain groceries from town, beautiful views
2. A H Dunas (shared room €15-20/person): Bernardo Álvarez Galán 1, 985502244
3. A Pez Escorpion (Hostel, 20, €20-25): Marola 1, 985500859, surf school
4. H Castillo de Gauzon (€44-60/55-77): Campón 22, 985502634
5. H Cactus B&B Salinas (€25/55+): Campón 58, 985500154, +400m

19.3 Soto del Barco H

H Palacio de la Magdalena (€75-135): Magdalena 50, 985588899, spa
H Rural Foncubierta (€50-70): Foncubierta, 985588418, +700m

22.8 Muros de Nalón A H

1. A La Naranja Peregrina (20, don): Era 27, 685245111, Apr-Oct, 200m before Casa Carmina
2. A H Casa Carmina (18, €14-15/30/45): Riego 21, 985583137/646135438, 12pm Apr-mid Oct
3. H Apartaments Turísticos la Flor (€55-80): Arango 28, 985583106
4. H Atico & Chic con Encanto (€45-70): Galicia 12C, 649739714
5. H Playa de Las Llanas (€70-110): Aldea Reborio 99B, 985583868, +900m

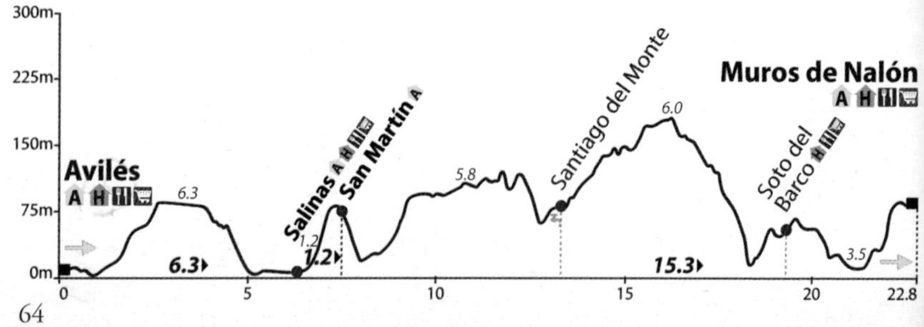

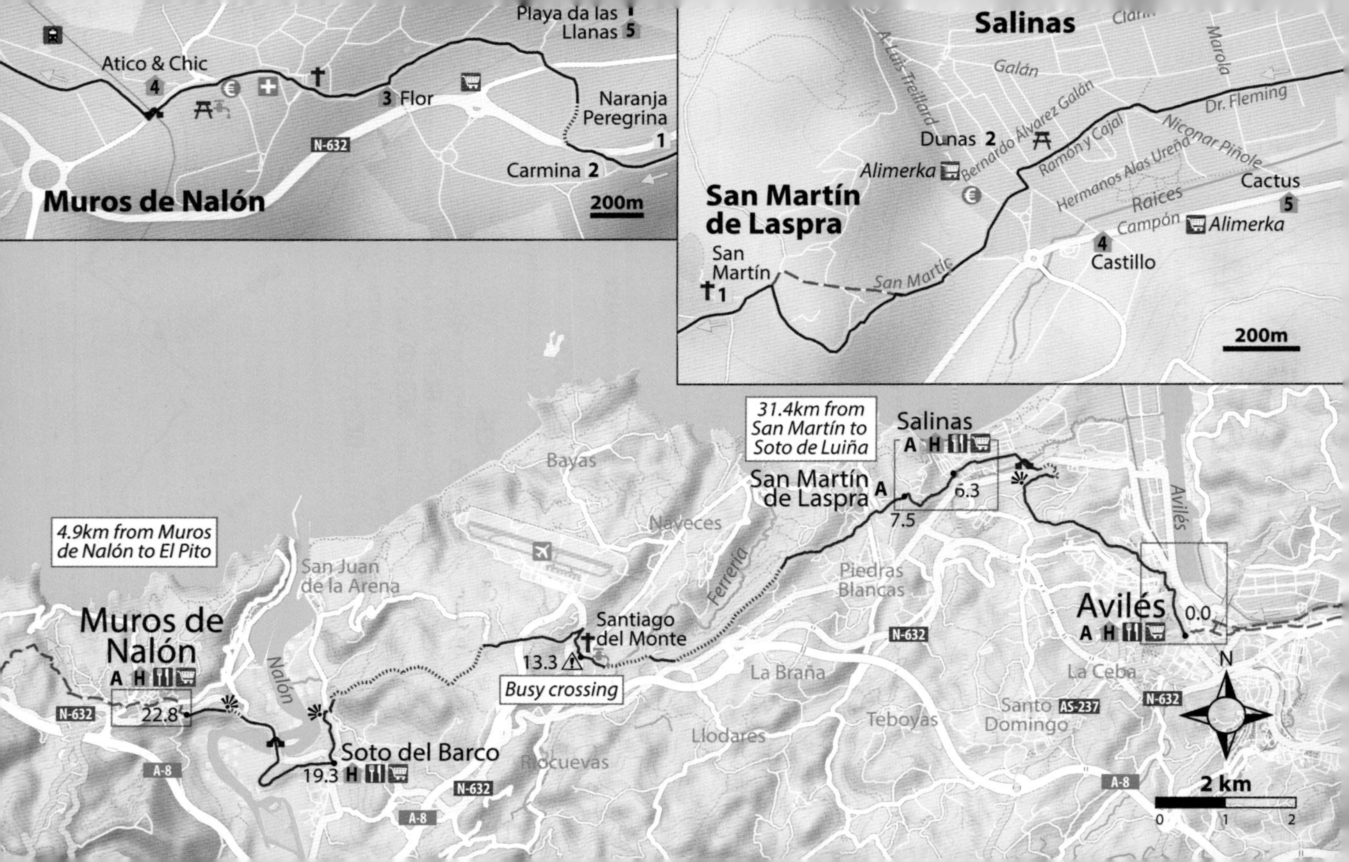

Muros de Nalón
Atico & Chic 4
Playa da las Llanas 5
3 Flor
Naranja Peregrina 1
Carmina 2
N-632
200m
Salinas
San Martín de Laspra
San Martín 1
A. Luis Treillard
Galán
Marola
Dr. Fleming
Dunas 2
Bernardo Álvarez Galán
Ramón y Cajal
Niconar Piñole
Hermanos Alas Ureña
Raices
Campón
Alimerka
Cactus 5
4 Castillo
San Martín
200m
31.4km from San Martín to Soto de Luiña
Salinas
San Martín de Laspra
6.3
7.5
Avilés
0.0
Bayas
Naveces
Ferrería
Piedras Blancas
4.9km from Muros de Nalón to El Pito
San Juan de la Arena
Muros de Nalón
22.8
Nalón
Santiago del Monte
13.3
Busy crossing
Soto del Barco
19.3
La Braña
La Ceba
Santo Domingo
AS-237
Teboyas
Llodares
Riocuevas
N-632
A-8
N
2 km
0
1
2

24 MUROS DE NALÓN TO SOTO DE LUIÑA

16.4km (10.2mi), 5-6.5 HOURS, DIFFICULTY:

P 67%, 11.0km, U 33%, 5.4km

While there is no one major climb between Muros de Nalón and Soto de Luiña, you'll be going up and down all day—views to the sea and the inland mountains are ample reward for your effort. With the day's manageable distance, you should arrive in Soto de Luiña in good time. There are not many services throughout the day, so plan accordingly. Soto de Luiña is a small town but has most essential services.

4.9 El Pito A H

1. A **Cudillero** (8, €12.50-25): , Av. de Selgas, 985590204
2. H **Álvaro** (€25/32+): , Av de Selgas, 985590204
3. H **Vitorio** (pil. rate shared room: €10, €35+/45+): , Av Selgas, 985591003
4. H **Apartamentos Cudillero** (pilgrim rate shared room €18/person, apartment €80+): , Barrio el Pito, 627570267
5. H **Aguilar** (€55-120): , Barrio el Pito, 985590582
6. H **Casona Selgas** (€40-100): , Av de Selgas, 985590548

7.3 San Juan de Piñera H

All services 500m or more off route.

H **Lupa** (€40-45/55-65): , Ctra N-632 Km 122, 985590973, +500m

9.5 El Rellayo H

H **Casa Fernanda II** (€30-40/50-65): , 985590292

10.9 Playa de Concha de Artedo H

H **Pensión Casa Miguel** (€50-60): , Playa de La Concha de Artedo, 985596350

16.4 Soto de Luiña A H

1. A **Municipal** (48, €5): , 985596283 all year
2. H **Casa Vieja del Sastre** (€40-90/50-110): , Los Quintos, 985596190
3. H **Paulino** (€15-20/25-30 shared bath): , Los Quintos, 985596038
4. H **La Hortona** (€40-100): , Plaza Principe de Asturias, 985596760
5. H **Valle Las Luiñas** (€44-66/55-88): , Crta General, 985596283

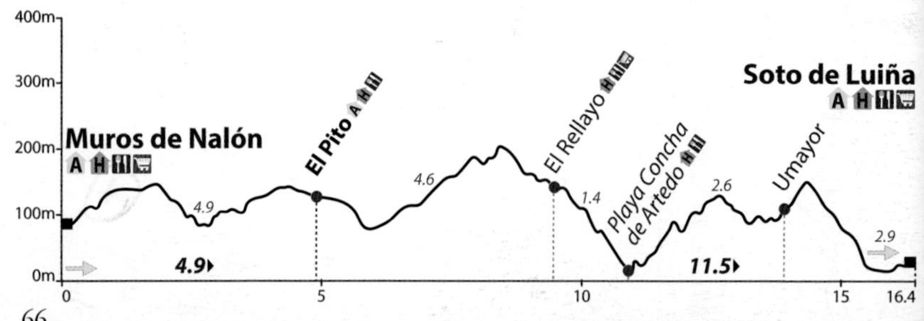

Soto de Luiña
N-632a
1 Municipal
5 Valle Las Luiñas
Register for albergue in Café Ecu
Ecu
4 Hortona
Esqueiro
Soto de Luiña
Paulino 3
Vieja del Sastre 2
100m
Palacio Segías
Cudillero 1
Álvaro 2 (same location)
5 Aguilar
Vitorio 3
El Pito
N-632
Apt. Cudillero 4
100m
Esqueiro
A-8
Playa Concha deArtedo
Soto de Luiña
16.4
N-632a
El Rellayo
Lamuño
10.9
9.5
Cudiullero
La Atalaya
Dangerous crossing
N-632
El Pito
La Magdalena
Umayor
N-632a
Artedo
13.5
7.3
San Juan de Piñera
Lupa
4.9
Reborio
Muros de Nalón
Castañedo
N
1.5 km
0
0.75
1.5
A-8
N-632
0.0

25 SOTO DE LUIÑA TO CADAVEDO

18.9km (11.7mi), **6-7.5 Hours, Difficulty:**
53%, 10.1km, 47%, 8.8km

From Soto de Luiña, there are two route options to Cadavedo. Shortly after passing the traffic circle and immediately after Hotel Cabo Vidío, the **route splits.** Both options are lovely with a healthy dose of up and down. ❶ A northern option (turn R) via Ballota stays closer to the coast, following dirt tracks and paved roads. The route descends and ascends a number of steep valleys, several of which lead close to pristine, secluded beaches (only 100m less climbing than the official option). On this way, there are and A H. ❷ The "official" route turns left and follows dirt road/paths along the mountain ridge S of the coast and highway N-632a. There are no services before reaching Cadavedo, as well as significant climbs reaching 635m with spectacular views worth the challenge. At the end of this option, shortly after AS-268, marks lead on dirt paths passing west of Cadavedo to Villademoros (for Cadavedo, continue on AS-268).

5.1 Novellana H

H **El Fornón** (€40-60): , 985598025, additional pilgrim discounts

9.1 Santa Marina A H

A H **Pensión Prada** (40, €15/30/45): , N-632 16, 985598184,
all year, pilgrim dorm price in double room, check-in at Bar Gayo

11.8 Ballota A H

A H **Casa Fernando** (6, €13/25-30/40-55): , N-632 Km 147, 985598264
H **Casa Entrefaros** (house for 5 persons €100): , N-632 km 138, 630214722

18.9 Cadavedo / Villademoros A H

1. A **Municipal** (12, €6): , Antiguo General, 653128642, renovated
2. A H **Covi y Peter** (8, €15/-/25): , Corradas 7, 660147482, Easter-Oct
3. A H **Ina** (10, €15/-/30): , 626081451, dorm price in shared room
4. H **Casa Family Astour** (€30/37): , Los Campos 44, 622898387, +500m
5. H **Apartamentos la Regalina** (€69): , Ctra de la Playa, 985645056, +400m
6. H **Casa Roja** (€60-80): , Ctra de la Playa, 985244493
7. H **Astur Regal** (€40/70): , Millares, 985645777, +1km
8. H **Apartamentos Casa Carin** (5 pax apt €70+): , Lugar Villademoros, 985645078

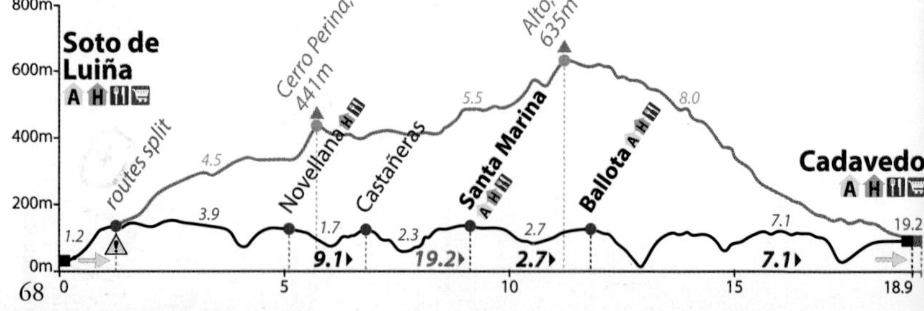

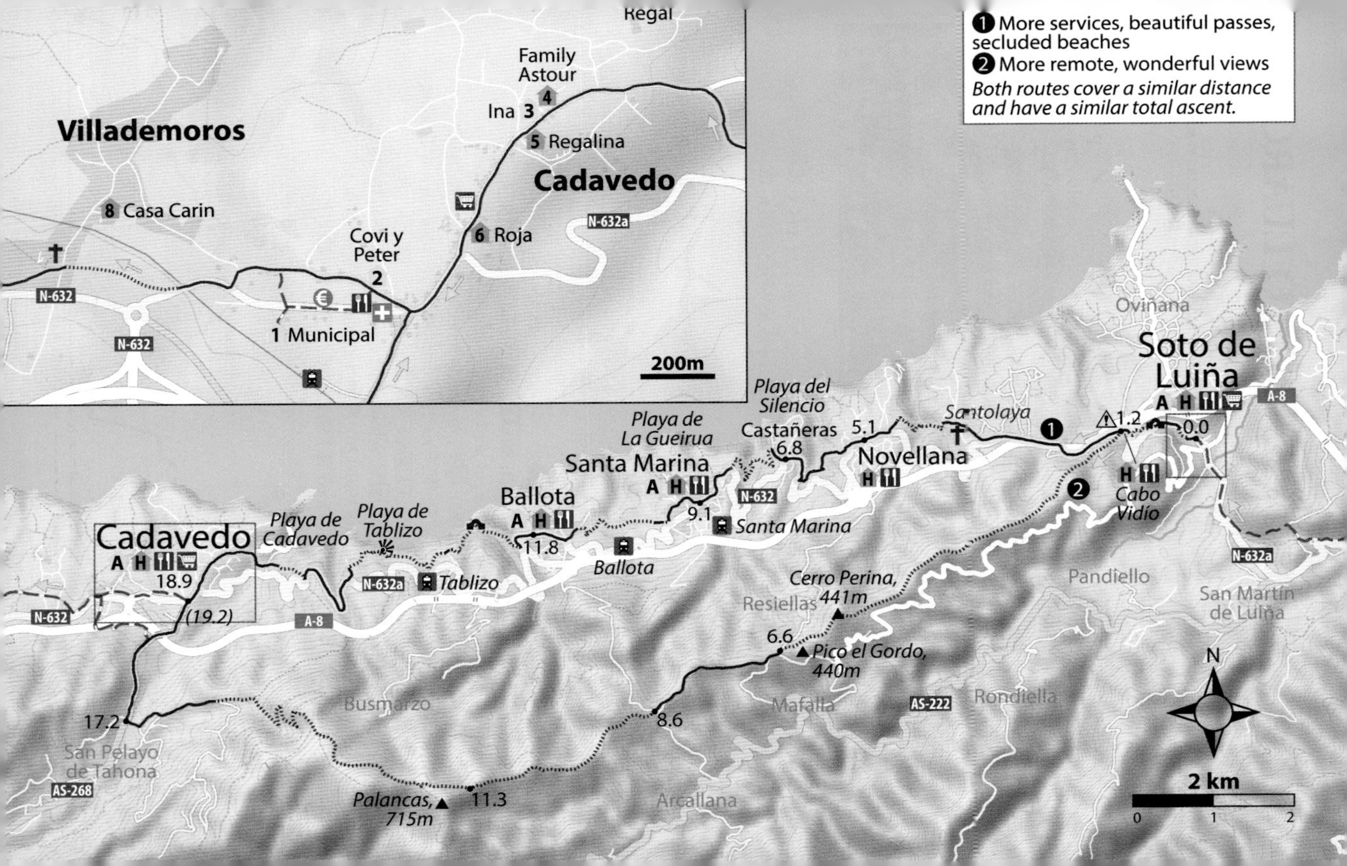

❶ More services, beautiful passes, secluded beaches
❷ More remote, wonderful views
Both routes cover a similar distance and have a similar total ascent.
Regal
Family Astour
4
Ina 3
5 Regalina
Villademoros
Cadavedo
8 Casa Carin
Covi y Peter
2
6 Roja
N-632a
N-632
1 Municipal
200m
Ovinana
Soto de Luiña
A-8
Playa del Silencio
Playa de La Gueirua
Castañeras
6.8
5.1
Santolaya
1
1.2
0.0
Santa Marina
Novellana
N-632
9.1
Santa Marina
2
Cabo Vidío
Ballota
11.8
Playa de Cadavedo
Playa de Tablizo
Cadavedo
18.9
(19.2)
N-632a
Tablizo
Ballota
N-632a
Pandiello
San Martín de Luiña
Cerro Perina, 441m
Resiellas
A-8
6.6
Pico el Gordo, 440m
N
17.2
Busmarzo
Mafalla
AS-222
Rondiella
8.6
San Pelayo de Tahona
AS-268
Palancas, 715m
11.3
Arcallana
2 km
0
1
2

26

CADAVEDO TO LUARCA

16.0km (9.9mi), **4.5-5.5 HOURS, DIFFICULTY:**
P 68%, 10.9km, U 32%, 5.1km

A pleasant, relatively flat stage. Navigation is overall straightforward. To reach the A municipal in Almuña, continue on N-634 when the official Camino route turns R to Barcia. From this point, it's another 3.3km to the albergue. If you intend to stay in the private albergue in Luarca, call in advance, as there are no other albergues in town.

8.4 Canero A H

A Playa Cueva (18, €10-12): Ctra N-634 KM 495.8, 985475036
H Canero (€20-40/35-60): Ctra N-634 Km 495.8, 985475036

13.0 Barcia H

H Casa la Fonte (€38-58): Barrio de Soledad, 985641896, 5% pilgrim discount

(14.8) Almuña A (On detour)

A Municipal (22, €5): Ctra AS-220, 985645320/650218326, all year, +1km
H Zabala (€60): Ctra. 634 km 503, 985640208

16.0 Luarca A H

1. **A Villa de Luarca** (22, €11-12): Álvaro de Albornoz 3, 660819434, all year, albergue across from hotel, inquire at hotel
2. **H Villa de Luarca** (€45/52-86): Álvaro de Albornoz 6, 985470703
3. **H La Colmena** (35-55/50-75): Uria 2, 985640278, 20% pilgrim discount
4. **H Rico** (€47-70): Plaza Alfonso X 6, 985470559
5. **H Dabeleira** (€35-45/40-80): Nicanor del Campo 12, 684630098
6. **H Casona El Gurugu** (€69-89/80-120): La Peña 93, 985470613
7. **H Báltico** (€55/65+): Paseo de Muelle 1, 985640991

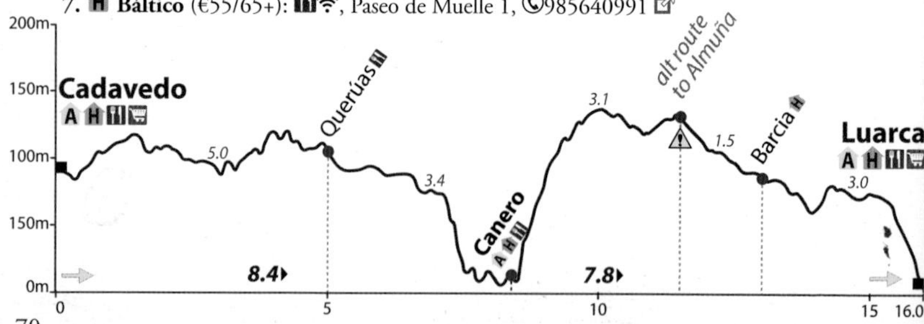

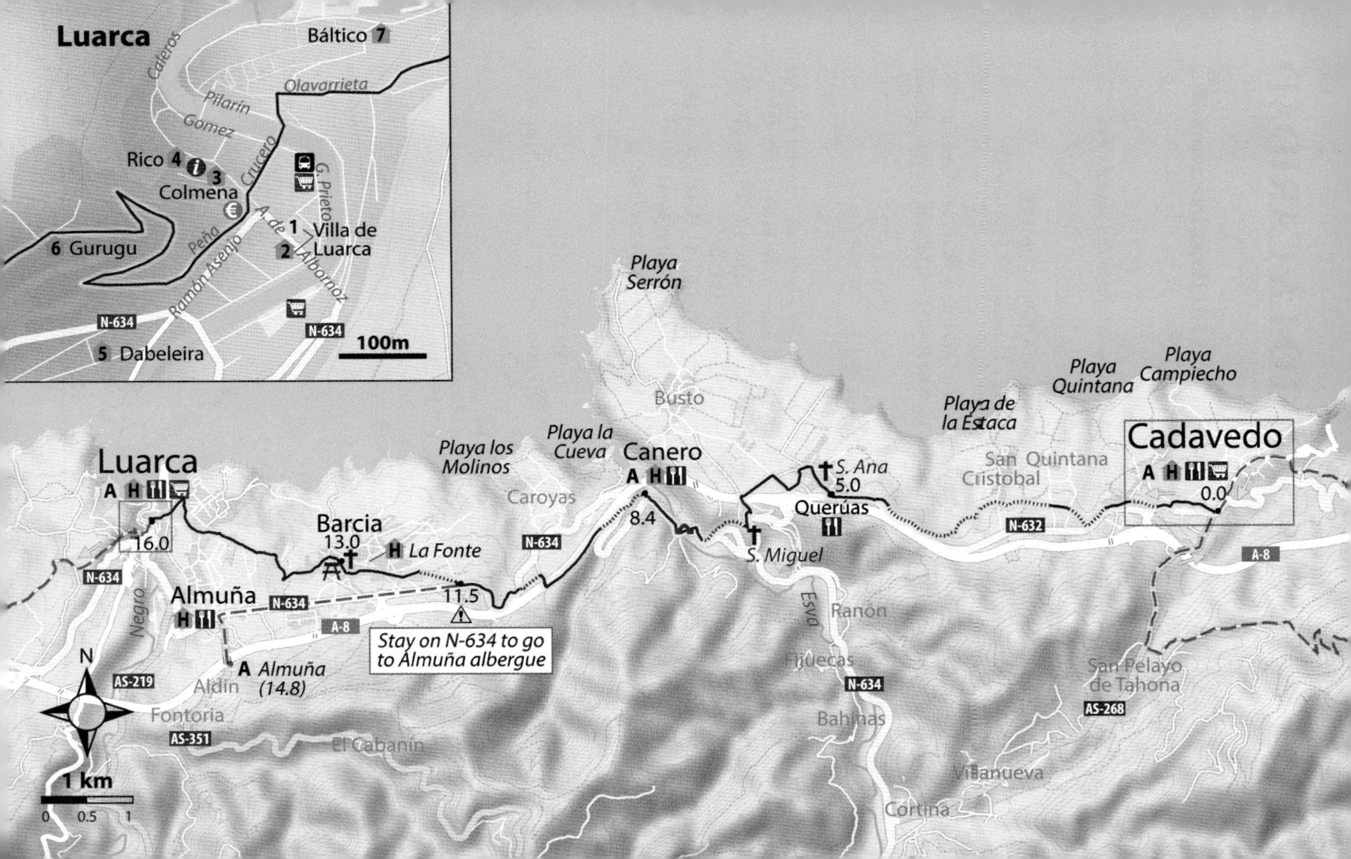

Luarca
Báltico 7
Caleros
Olavarrieta
Pilarín
Gomez
Rico 4
3
Colmena
Crucero
G. Prieto
1 Villa de Luarca
2
A. de Albornoz
Peña
Ramón Asenjo
6 Gurugu
N-634
5 Dabeleira
100m
Playa Serrón
Busto
Playa Campiecho
Playa Quintana
Playa de la Estaca
Cadavedo
0.0
San Cristobal
Quintana
N-632
A-8
S. Ana
5.0
Querúas
S. Miguel
Esva
Ranón
Fijuecas
Bahinas
San Pelayo de Tahona
AS-268
Villanueva
Cortina
Canero
8.4
Playa la Cueva
Playa los Molinos
Caroyas
Luarca
16.0
Barcia
13.0
La Fonte
11.5
Stay on N-634 to go to Almuña albergue
Almuña
Almuña (14.8)
Negro
Aldín
AS-219
Fontoria
AS-351
El Cabanín
N
1 km
0
0.5
1

27 LUARCA TO LA CARIDAD

30.2km (18.8mi), **8.5-11 Hours, Difficulty:**
P 71%, 21.4km, U 29%, 8.8km

Rural terrain dotted with small towns with occasional climbs and coastal views.

12.6 Villapedre H

H **El Pinar** (€34-39/40-50): N-634 km 516, 985472005
H **Villa Auristela** (€40-45/50-75): La Llamiella, 655846206

15.3 Piñera A

Few services, closest is 1km before A at N-634 crossing.
A **Municipal** (20, €5): N-634, 611040517, all year, communal meal

18.7 La Colorada H

H **Blanco** (€60-130): 985630775, spa

20.1 Navia A H

Nice place for a late lunch or to end a shorter day.

1. A **San Roque** (24, €10): Manuel Suárez 3, 691904242, Mar-Nov
2. H **Pensión Cantábrico** (€25-50/40-65): Mariano Luiña 12, 985474376
3. H **Arco Navia** (€50-75): San Francisco 2, 985473495
4. H **Palacio Arias** (€60-64/90-104): Emigrantes 11, 985473671
5. H **La Barca** (€25-40/38-75): Manuel Suárez 23, 618836141
6. H **Casona Naviega** (€45-60/55-80): Emigrantes 37, 985474880

26.6 Cartavio H

H **Mayce** (€20-30/30-40): N-634 km 530, 985478026
H **Casa El Nido de Olvido** (€55-75): Esteler, 651678696, Holy Week-Oct

30.2 La Caridad A H

1. A **Municipal** (18, €5): Av. Asturias, 685154405, all year
2. A H **Xana** (16, €11/-/30+): Asturias 18, 984196830, Jan-Oct
3. H **Pensión Sayane** (€23-35): Galicia 6, 985478229
4. H **Rural Casa Xusto** (€70-110): Prendones 8, 985154405

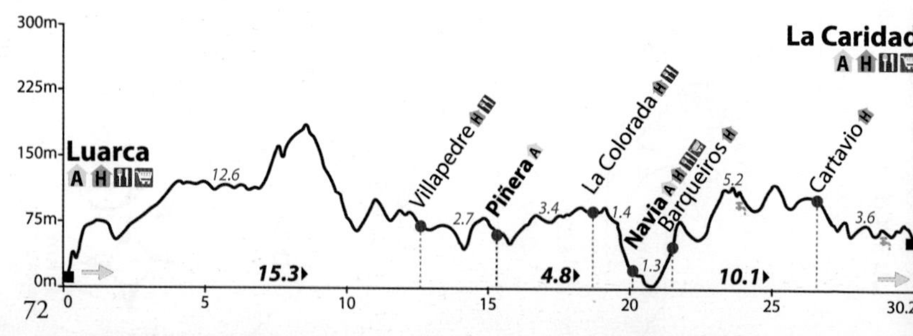

La Caridad
Galicia
Prendonés
Puerto
S. Miguel
Asturias
4 Xusto
3 Sayane
Xana 2
Padre Montaña
Covadonga
Municipal
1
100m
N-634
Barqueiros
Navia
Meiro
AS-12
100m
Cantábrico
R. de Campamor
2
1
S. Roque
Arco 3
N-634
Navia
Arias 4
Emigrantes
Manuel
Suárez
5
Barca
Naviega 6
La Caridad
A H
N-634
30.2
A-8
Miudeira
Cartavio
H
El Nido de Olvido
26.6
25.1
H
Careful walking along N-634
Ortiguera
Navia
A H
N-634
20.1
18.7
Las Cortinas
H
La Colorada
A-8
AS-12
Coaña
Navia
Armental
Sante
Anleo
Villacondide
Ansilan
Arancedo
15.3
A
Piñera
Puerto de Vega
Villapedre
H
12.6
Somorto
Barayo
Las Barqueras
N-634
Boronas
La Artosa
El Vallín
Villuir
Luarca
A H
0.0
Santiago
N-634
A-8
Setienes
Negro
N
2 km
0
1
2

28 LA CARIDAD TO RIBADEO

22.8km (14.2mi), **6.5-8.5 Hours, Difficulty:**
88%, 20.1km, 12%, 2.7km

Last day in Asturias and on the coast before route turns inland after Ribadeo.

5.8 Porcía H **Apartamentos Porcía** (€55-110): , Campos, 985977207

10.8 Tapia de Casariego A H; A in great location over rugged beach!
1. A **Municipal** (30, €8): , S. Martín, 985471099, ocean views, neglected
2. H **Puente de los Santos** (€25+/40+): , Galicia 15, 985628155
3. H **La Ruta** (€28+/39+): , Galicia 4, 985628138
4. H **San Antón** (€35-50/50-75): , San Blas 2, 985628000

17.1 Playa de Peñarronda H
H **Parajes** (€40+): , 985979050

20.2 Figueras A H
1. A H **Camino Norte** (16, €12-15/30/40+): , 985636207, Feb-Oct
2. H **Casa Peleyón** (€45-95/65-110): , Lois, 676700778
3. H **Palacete Peñalba**: , Granda, 677516397, historic building

22.8 Ribadeo A H Great A with few beds overlooking river!
1. A **Xunta** (12, €6): , 982128689, a. y., N of bridge, call for code to key box
2. A H **Santa Cruz** (25, €10/25/40): , 637458654
3. H **A.G. Porcillán** (€40-50/55-85): , Puerto de Porcillán, 982120570
4. H **Fogar do Mariñeiro** (€50-82): , Muelle de Porcillán, 982120042
5. H **Ponte Dos Santos** (€27+/35+): , Rosalía Castro 18, 982130629
6. H **Rolle** (€60-98): , Ingeniero Schultz 6, 982120670
7. H **Mediante** (€30-50/50-70): , España 16, 982130453
8. H **Pensión Linares** (€44-57): , España 13, 982129633
9. H **Costa Verde** (€20-24/36-50): , España 11, 696885639
10. H **Pensión Orol** (€15-20/25-35): , San Francisco 9, 982128742
11. H **Bouza** (€55-80): , José Vicente Pérez Martínez 13, 982130087
12. H **Parador** (€75-204): , Amador Fernández 7, 982128825

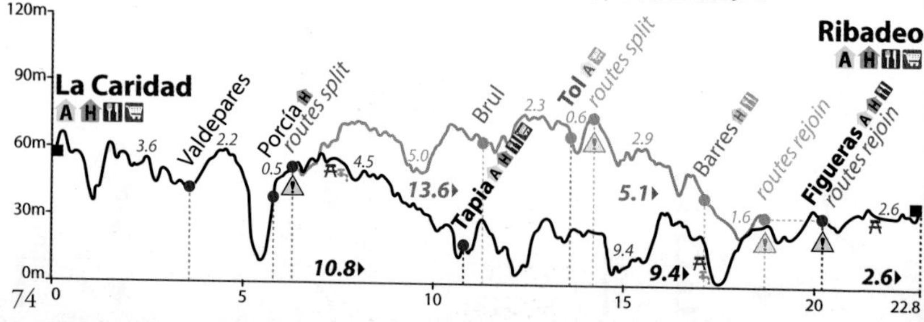

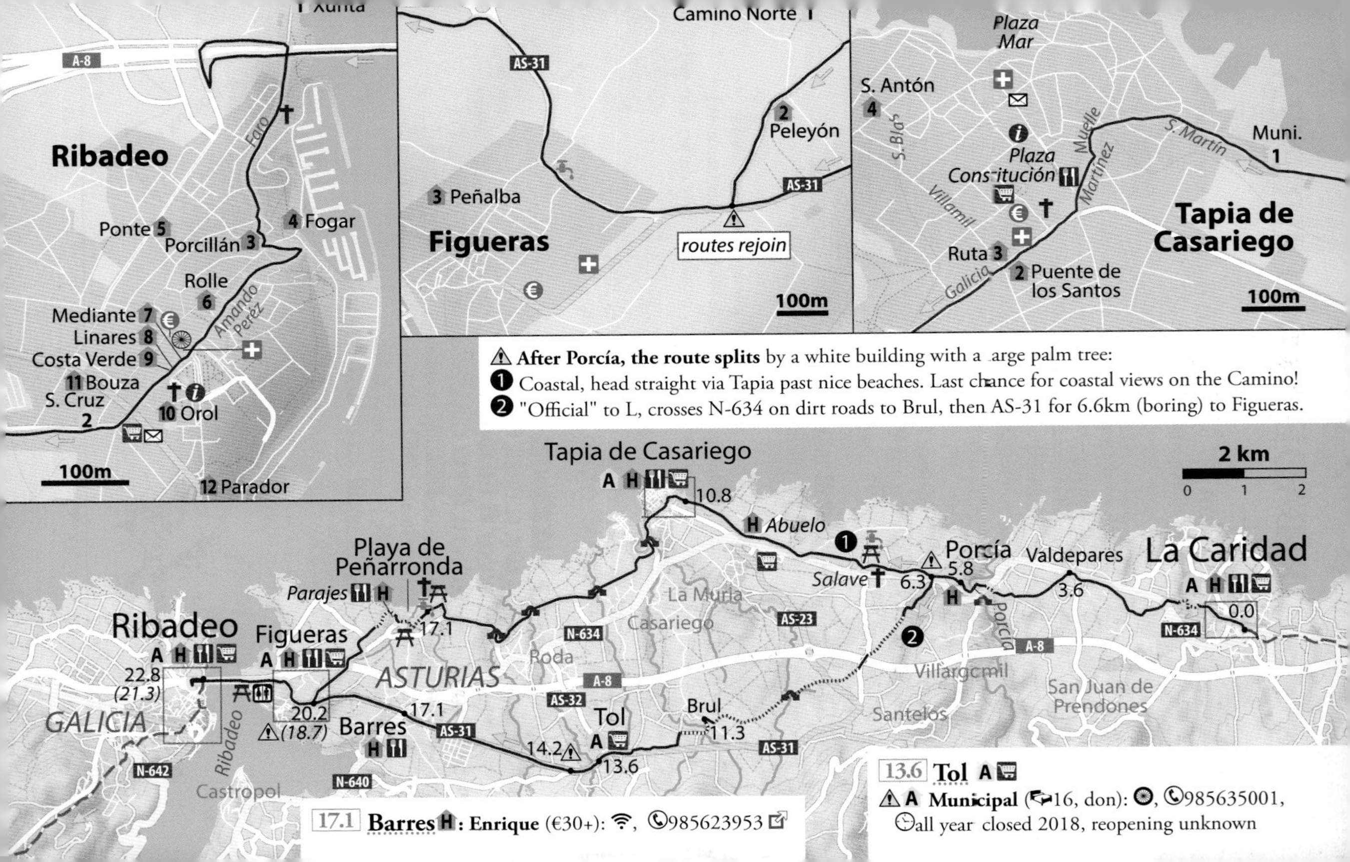

⚠ **After Porcía, the route splits** by a white building with a large palm tree:

❶ Coastal, head straight via Tapia past nice beaches. Last chance for coastal views on the Camino!

❷ "Official" to L, crosses N-634 on dirt roads to Brul, then AS-31 for 6.6km (boring) to Figueras.

17.1 **Barres** H: **Enrique** (€30+): wifi, ✆985623953

13.6 **Tol** A

⚠ A **Municipal** (16, don): ✆985635001, all year closed 2018, reopening unknown

29 RIBADEO TO LOURENZÁ

28.6km (17.8mi), 8.5-11 Hours, Difficulty:
P 70%, 20.0km, U 30%, 8.6km

From Ribadeo, say goodbye to the coast (and flat terrain) and head inland through sparsely-populated forested hill-country—a pretty journey with wonderful views. There are few services along the way before Lourenzá, so restock in Ribadeo. (Don't count on the café in Vilela being open early.) If planning to stay in Xunta albergues in Gondán or San Xusto, be aware that there are no grocery stores nearby (and limited food options).

7.7 Vilela A
A **Municipal** (22, €5): , Antiguas Escuelas, 982128689, renovated 2017
A **A Pena** (12, €10): , Crtra Vilela-Cubelas Km 7, 982137629
H **Casa Domingo** (€25/35+): , San Vicente, 982137449, 2km after Vilela

19.7 Vilamartín Grande H
The lovely little café makes a nice break spot.
H **Tentempé Peregrino** (€35+): , Villamartin Grande 9, 610451518

22.0 Gondán A
Picnic tables outside albergue make a good break spot.
⚠ A **Municipal** (14, don): , Lugar Gondan 30, 619515400, very basic and sometimes locked, isolated without shops or restaurants, possible to have dinner delivered from Bar A Curva in San Xusto

23.8 San Xusto A
The albergue was renovated in 2018.
A **Municipal** (14, don): , O Corveiro, 982144072, a. y., keys at Bar A Curva

28.6 Lourenzá A H A
Visit the beautiful San Salvador Monastery.
1. A **Xunta** (20, €6): , Pr. Gracia, 652186731, a. y., overflow in polideportivo
2. A **Savior** (24, €13/-/32): , , Calvo Sotelo 15, 982121496, Apr-Oct
3. A A **O Camiño** (12, €11): , Calvo Sotelo 3, 696570192, Apr-Oct
4. A **Castelos** (40, €12+/-/40): , Mondoñedo 26, 982100887, a. y.
5. H **Pensión Rego** (€20-25/30-40): , Isla Nova 17, 982141819
6. H **Casa Gloria** (€30/38): , Peregrín Otero 3, 982121119
7. H **Hostal La Unión:** (€40-50): , Val 16, 982121028

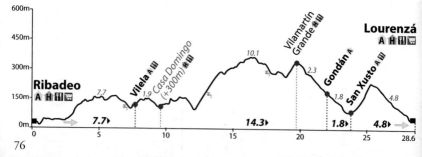

600m
450m
300m
150m
0m
Ribadeo A H
7.7
Vilela A
1.9 Casa Domingo (+300m) H
10.1
Vilamartín Grande H
2.3
Gondán A
1.8
San Xusto A
4.8
Lourenzá A H
7.7▸ 14.3▸ 1.8▸ 4.8▸
0 5 10 15 20 25 28.6

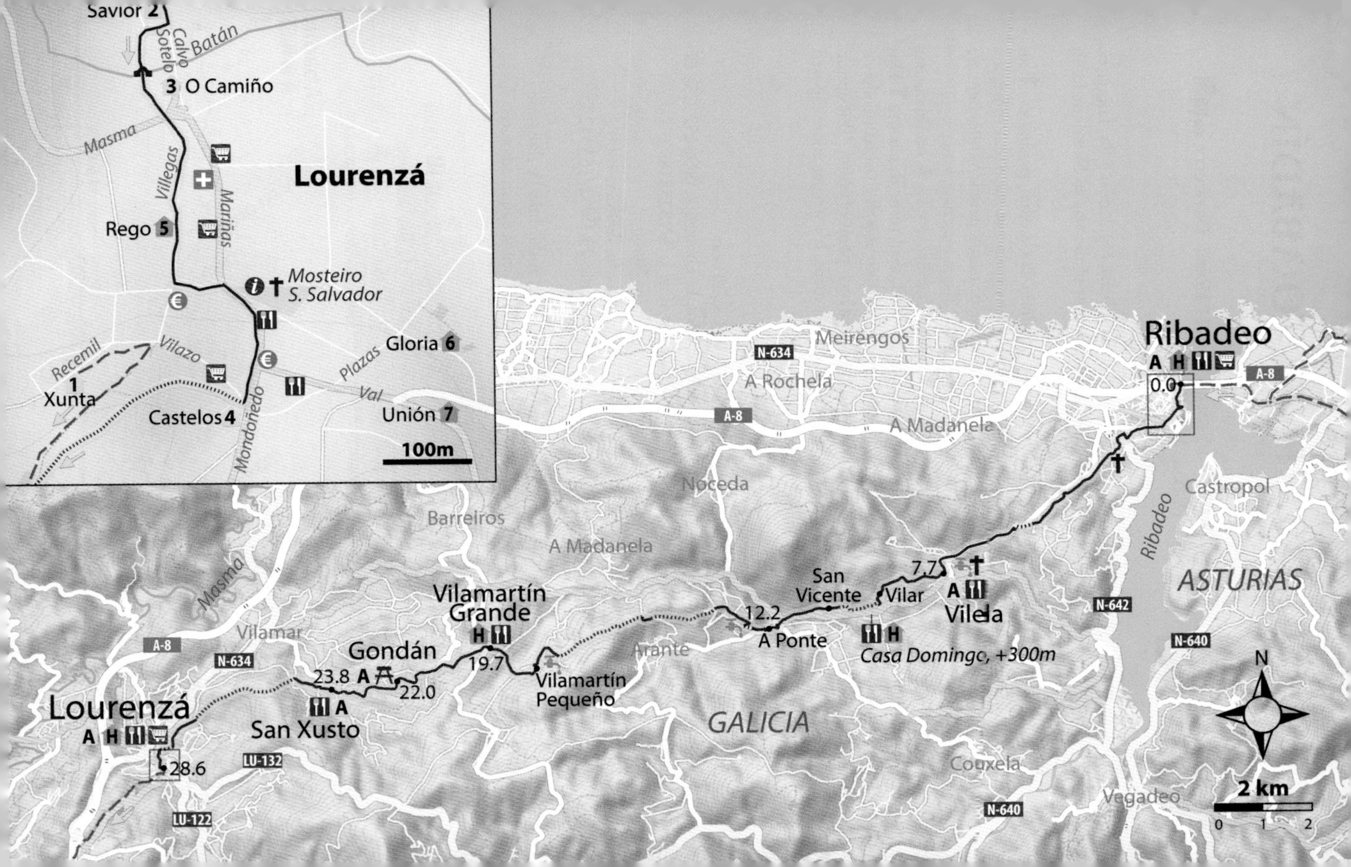

Savior 2
Calvo Sotelo
Batán
3 O Camiño
Masma
Villegas
Mariñas
Lourenzá
Rego 5
Mosteiro S. Salvador
Gloria 6
Recemil
Vilazo
Plazas
1 Xunta
Castelos 4
Mondoñedo
Val
Unión 7
100m
Ribadeo
0.0
A-8
N-634
Meirengos
A Rochela
A Madanela
Noceda
Castropol
Ribadeo
ASTURIAS
Barreiros
A Madanela
7.7
San Vicente
Vilar
Vilela
Masma
Vilamartín Grande
12.2
A Ponte
N-642
N-640
Vilamar
Gondán
Arante
Casa Domingo, +300m
A-8
N-634
23.8
19.7
22.0
Vilamartín Pequeño
Lourenzá
San Xusto
GALICIA
N
LU-132
28.6
Couxela
2 km
Vegadeo
N-640
LU-122
0
1
2

30 LOURENZÁ TO ABADÍN

27.2km (16.9mi), 8.5-11 Hours, Difficulty:
P 69%, 18.7km, U 31%, 8.5km

Enjoy wonderful views as you climb further into rural Galician highlands. From Lourenzá, follow the regional trail *Camino Natural de San Rosendo* most of the way to Mondoñedo. In Mondoñedo, the route splits at the Praza da Catedral:

❶ **Traditional** ("Camino Alternativo"): Go S across the Praza da Catedral, passing the ✝ on your L. Reach Fonte Vella and turn R, following paved roads up out of town and through a beautiful valley (Valiñadares River below on L). This route is mostly paved. While there are few services outside of the albergue in Maariz, a few small villages may have water.

❷ **Mountain** ("Official"): Newer route leaves the Praza da Catedral toward A on Rúa Leiras Pulpeiro. Past the A, the route follows Av. San Lucas L uphill, then turns R, passing ✝ Dos Remedios and crossing N-634a (first ➡ appears, afterwards route is well-marked). Follow a small road past Cesuras, and climb steeply on dirt roads to a high point of 680m. This option is 5.4km shorter, has wonderful views, and is mostly on dirt roads. It's steeper, more exposed to the sun, and has no services until Gontán.

8.9 Mondoñedo A H

1. A **Xunta** (22, €6): Valada 2, 982524003, all year
2. A H **Montero** (38, €15/28/45+): E. Lorenzo 7, 982521751
3. H **Hostal Padornelo** (€20/40+): Buenos Aires 1, 982521892
4. H **Central Hostal** (€25+): Andrés Baamonde 3, 676479600
5. H **Seminario Santa Catalina** (€21-27/30-44): Plaza Seminario, 982521000
6. H **Casa Bracamonte** (€45-50/50-58): Jose María Pardo 23, 629165342

11.6 Maariz A

- On Traditional Option ❶, A has snacks and drinks by donation

A ☆ **O Bisonte de Maariz** (6, don): 626766235, must call in advance

27.2 Abadín / Gontán A H

1. A **Xunta** (24, €6): Ctra Labrada, 616251462, all year, 500m
2. A **Xabarín** (26, €15): Galicia 28, 690181811, all year
3. A H **Goás** (30, €10/24/39): Galicia 23, 982508005, A in 2019
4. H **Pensión Niza** (€30+): Galicia 31, 982508032, closed on Sundays

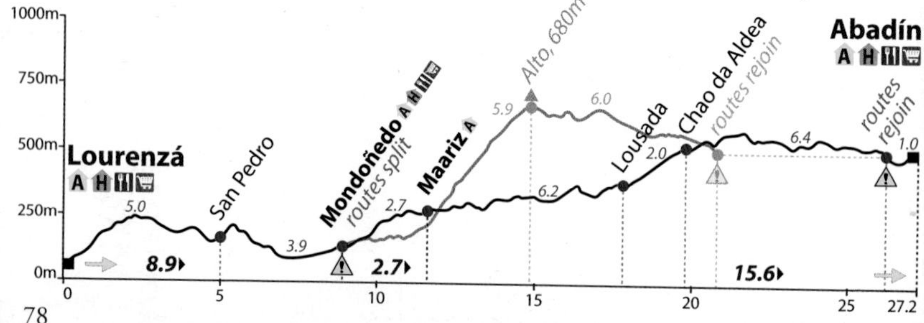

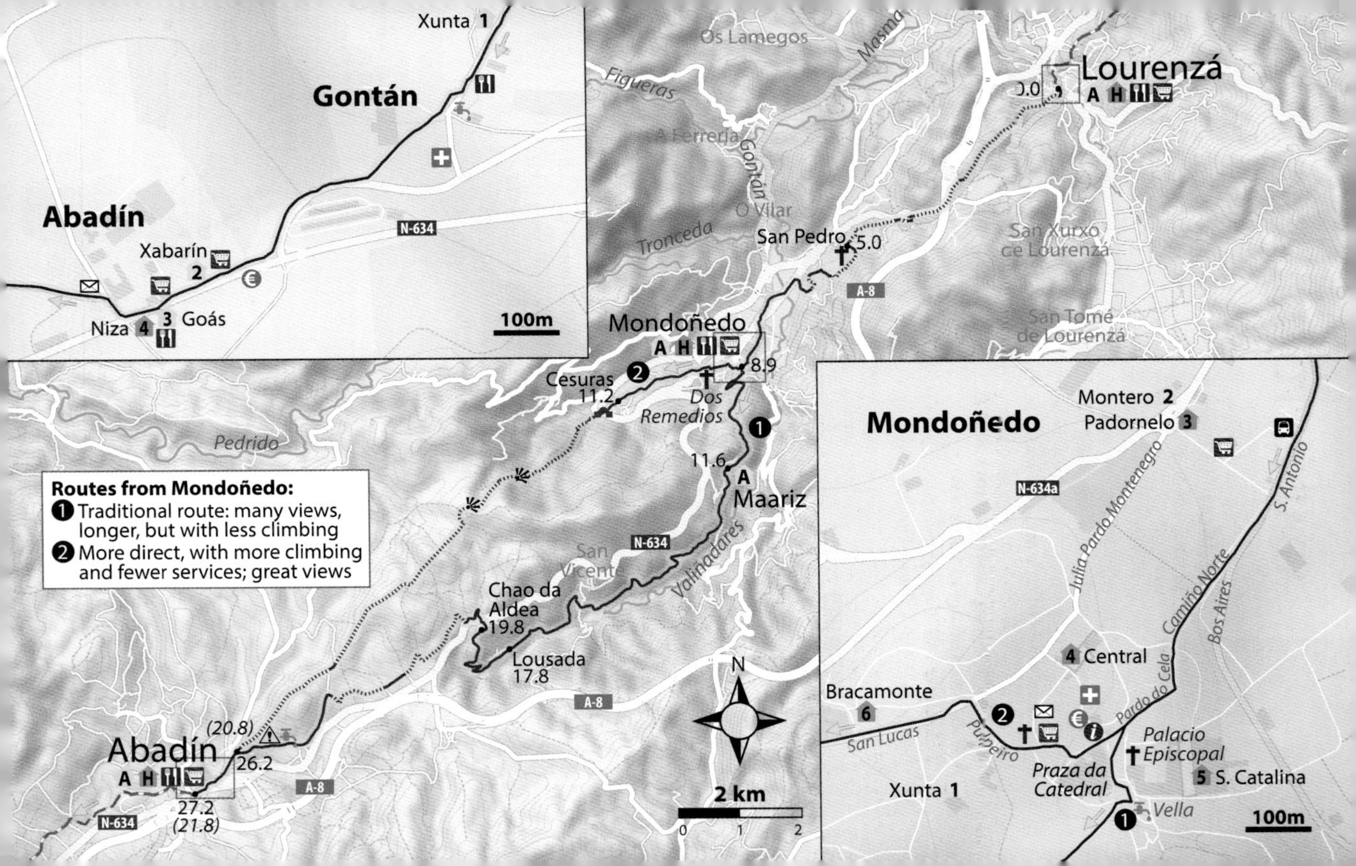

Gontán
Abadín
Xunta 1
Xabarín
2
3 Goás
Niza 4
N-634
100m
Lourenzá
A H
0.0
Os Lamegos
Masma
Figueras
A Ferrería
Gontán
O Vilar
Tronceda
San Pedro
5.0
San Xurxo de Lourenzá
San Tomé de Lourenzá
A-8
Mondoñedo
A H
8.9
Cesuras
11.2
Dos Remedios
11.6
A
Maariz
Pedrido
N-634
San Vicente
Valinadares
Chao da Aldea
19.8
Lousada
17.8
A-8
(20.8)
Abadín
A H
26.2
27.2
(21.8)
N-634
N
2 km
0
1
2
Routes from Mondoñedo:
1 Traditional route: many views, longer, but with less climbing
2 More direct, with more climbing and fewer services; great views
Mondoñedo
Montero 2
Padornelo 3
N-634a
Julia Pardo Montenegro
S. Antonio
Camiño Norte
Bos Aires
4 Central
Bracamonte
6
San Lucas
Pumeiro
Pardo do Cela
Palacio Episcopal
Praza da Catedral
5 S. Catalina
Xunta 1
Vella
100m

31

ABADÍN TO VILALBA

21.0km (13.0mi), 5.5-7 Hours, Difficulty:

P 47%, 9.9km, U 53%, 11.1km

A pleasant relatively-flat day of walking provides welcome respite after two hilly days. The route's general proximity to highway N-634 means access to several cafés along the way.

5.9 As Paredes (Castromaior)

O Xistral (14, €12/-/35): Lugar Paredes 35, 673524257, Easter-Nov rest of year by reservation

15.2 Goiriz

Hostal O Cristo (€20-30/35-40): N-634 km 619, 982527322

21.0 Vilalba

The Xunta is located 2.6km before the town center. There is a nearby, but no . If you plan to use the , consider carrying food from Abadín.

1. **Xunta** (48, €6): Polígono Industrial de Vilalba, 659494969, 1pm all year, 2.6km before town center
2. **As Pedreiras** (28, €10): Pita Veiga 4, 620137711, Mar-Nov
3. **Castelos** (38, €10): Pedreiras 16, 982100887, all year
4. **Hostal Terra Chá** (€28-31/39-46): Domingo Goás 10, 982511702
5. **Vila do Alba** (€35/45): Campo de Puente 27-29, 982510245
6. **Venezuela** (€22-27/35-40): Plaza Suso Gayoso 10, 982510659
7. **Parador** (€60-120): C. Valeriano Valdesuso, 982510011

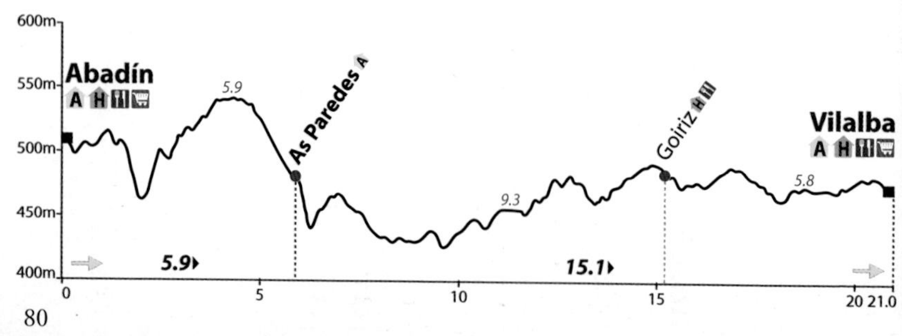

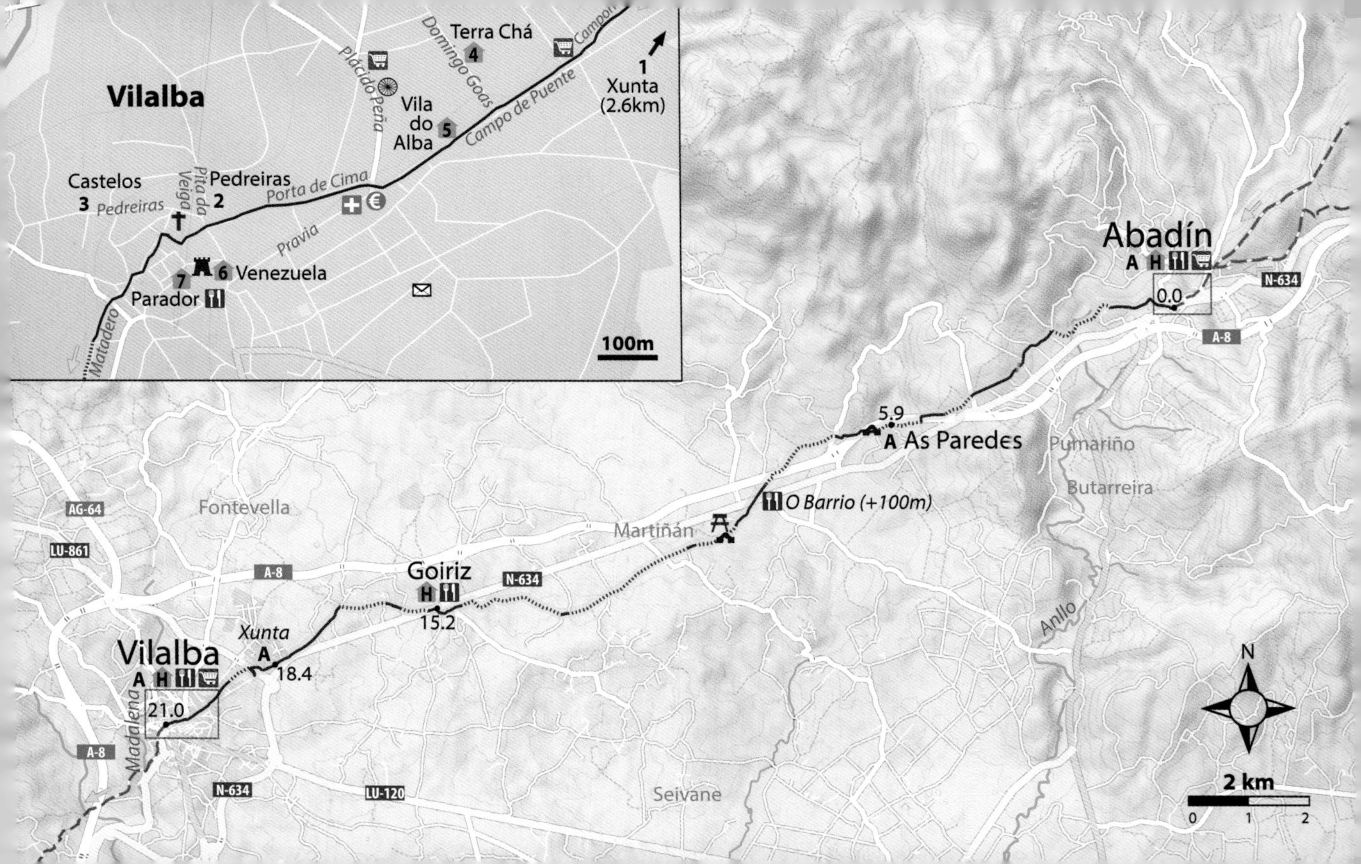
Vilalba
Terra Chá
4
Domingo Goas
Plácido Peña
Vila do Alba
5
Campo de Puente
1
Xunta (2.6km)
Castelos
3
Pedreiras
Pita da Veiga
Pedreiras
2
Porta de Cima
Pravia
7
6
Venezuela
Parador
Matadero
100m
Abadín
A H
N-634
0.0
A-8
5.9
A As Paredes
Pumariño
Butarreira
O Barrio (+100m)
Martiñán
Fontevella
AG-64
LU-861
A-8
Goiriz
H
N-634
15.2
Xunta
A
18.4
Vilalba
A H
21.0
Madalena
A-8
N-634
LU-120
Seivane
Anllo
N
2 km
0
1
2

32 VILALBA TO BAAMONDE

18.6km (11.6mi), 5-6 Hours, Difficulty:
P 59%, 10.9km, U 41%, 7.7km

Easy walking to Baamonde, which offers a well-maintained Xunta A with ample space at 94. Baamonde, while small, has all basic services. It's the last place you'll find a stand-alone grocery store before Sobrado dos Monxes, so stock up with food here. For a longer day, consider walking on to Miraz. It's a long day from Vilalba (33.6km) but relatively flat.

18.6 Baamonde

1. **A Xunta** (94, €6): Crta Vilalba 9, 628250323, 1pm all year
2. **H Hostal Ruta Esmeralda** (€35+): Ctra N-VI, Km 529.6, 982398138, mixed reviews, gas station, car garage and restaurant complex

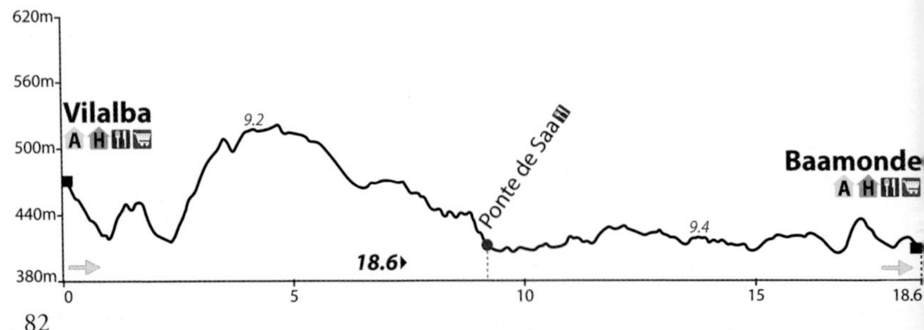

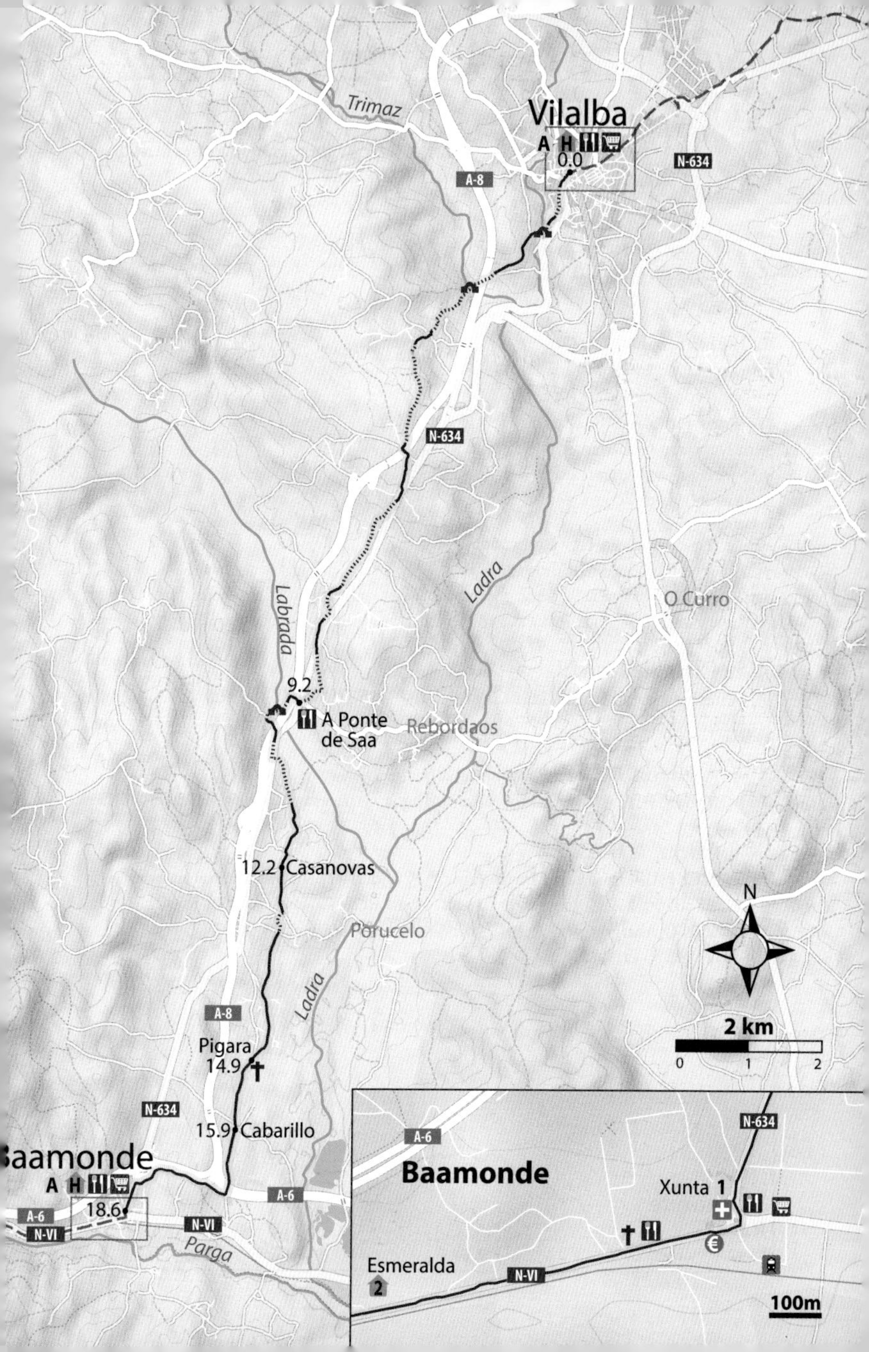

Trimaz
Vilalba
A H
0.0
A-8
N-634
N-634
Labrada
Ladra
O Curro
9.2
A Ponte
de Saa
Rebordaos
12.2 Casanovas
Porucelo
N
Ladra
A-8
2 km
0
1
2
Pigara
14.9
N-634
15.9 Cabarillo
Baamonde
A H
18.6
A-6
A-6
N-VI
N-VI
Parga
A-6
N-634
Baamonde
Xunta 1
Esmeralda
2
N-VI
100m

33

BAAMONDE TO MIRAZ

15.0km (9.3mi), 4-5 Hours, Difficulty: ▬□□
P 68%, 10.2km, U 32%, 4.8km

This stage traverses more isolated areas passing through a handful of small villages before Sobrado dos Monxes.

⚠ The **route splits** at 5.2km.
❶ Stay L for the traditional route to Miraz (recommended).
❷ A new route goes R, shaving around 9km from the total remaining distance to Santiago; but there are few if any services in this direction.

While there are no grocery stores today, A A Lagoa has a small shop, and A San Martín in Miraz sells basic food supplies to pilgrims staying there. For a longer day, consider continuing to A Roxica, another 10.1km. Call ahead as there are only 10 beds.

9.5 Carballedo A

A **Witericus** (9, €12): , 678415728/982163095, Feb-mid Dec, peaceful location

13.1 A Lagoa A Small shop in albergue

A **A Lagoa** (16, €10): , , A Lagoa Carretera de Friol, 982153431

15.0 Miraz A H A

1. A A **CSJ Albergue San Martín** (asoc, 26, don): , Corral da Fonte, 982830700, 2:30pm Easter to Oct, operated by Confraternity of Saint James in UK
2. A H A **Ó Abrigo** (40, €10/-/40): , Lugar As Laxes 2, 982194850, all year

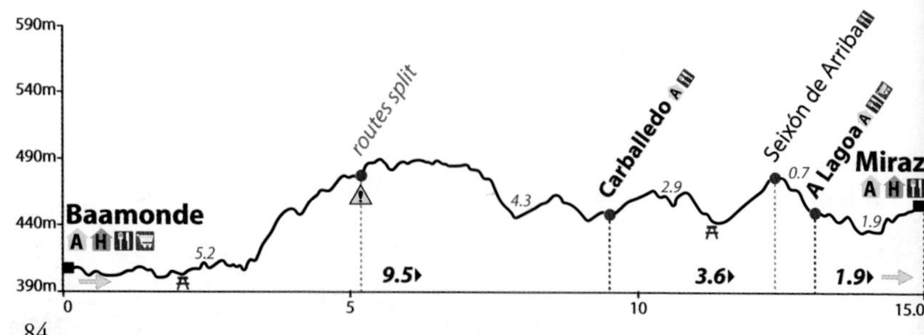

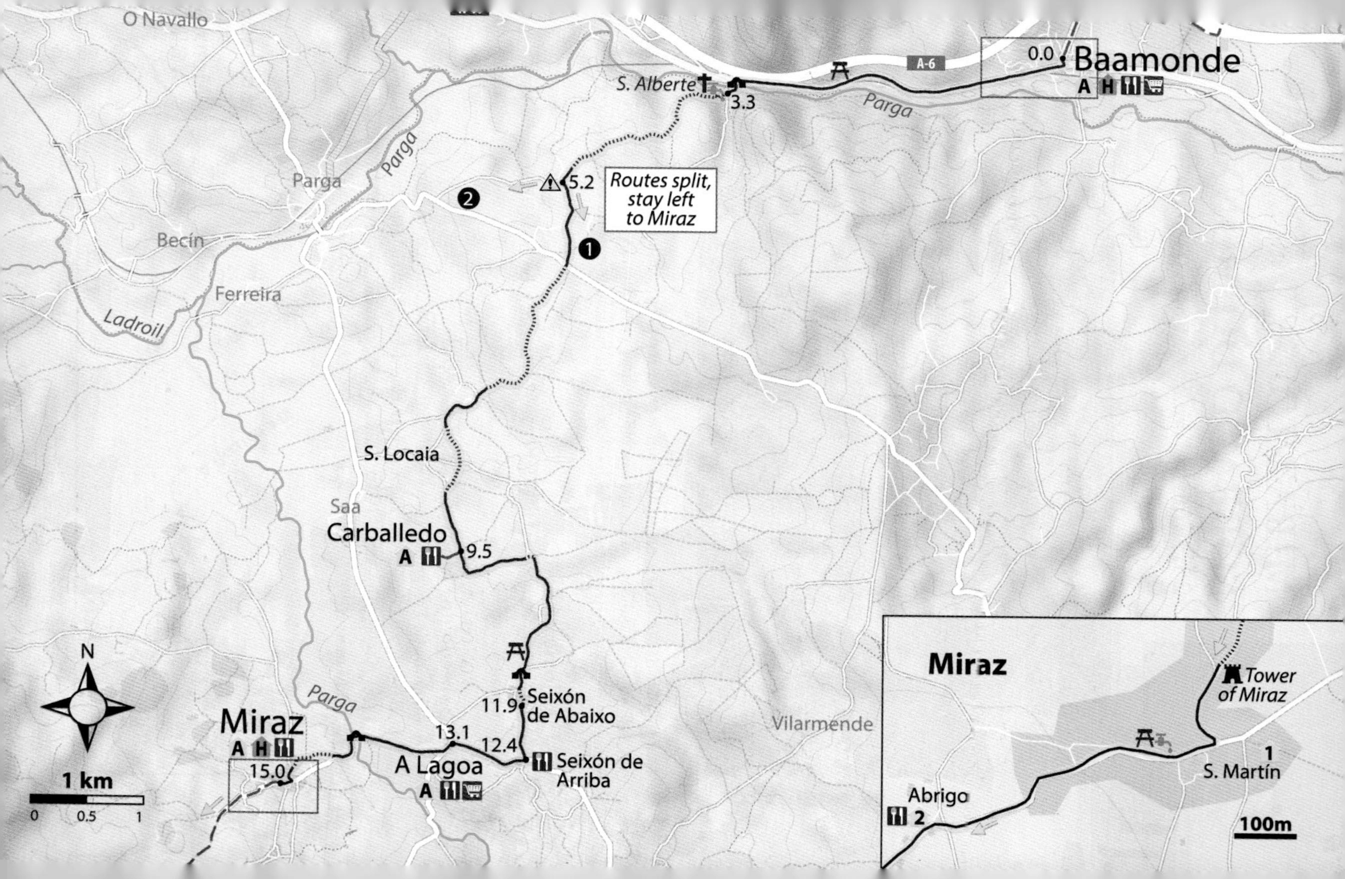

O Navallo
0.0
Baamonde
A H
A-6
S. Alberte
3.3
Parga
Routes split, stay left to Miraz
5.2
Parga
Becín
Ferreira
Ladroil
S. Locaia
Saa
Carballedo
A
9.5
Seixón de Abaixo
11.9
Seixón de Arriba
12.4
13.1
A Lagoa
A
Vilarmende
Parga
Miraz
A H
15.0
N
1 km
0
0.5
1
Miraz
Tower of Miraz
1
S. Martín
Abrigo
2
100m

34 MIRAZ TO SOBRADO DO MONXES

25.3km (15.7mi), 7-9 Hours, Difficulty:
P 67%, 17.0km, U 33%, 8.3km

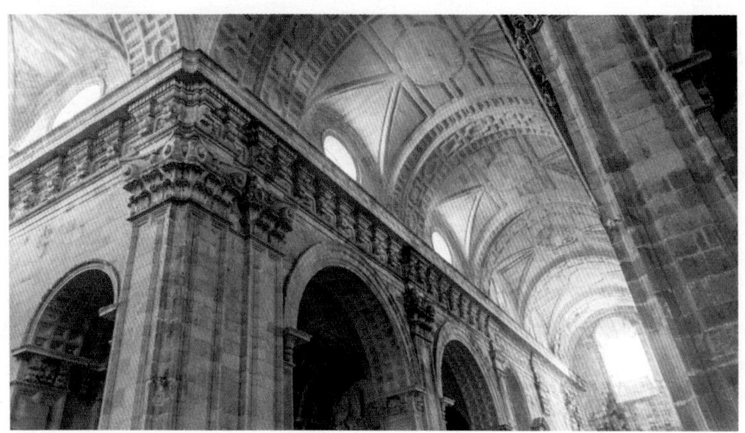

Enjoyable day of rural walking, far from services and people, although the route occasionally follows more built-up roads approaching Sobrado dos Monxes. Be sure to explore the stunning monastery in Sobrado, which offers a beautiful (and somewhat austere) albergue.

10.1 A Roxica A

A Casa Roxica (10, €11): Lugar a Roxica 2, 630487008, Mar-Dec, communal dinner

25.3 Sobrado dos Monxes A H

1. A **Albergue de Peregrinos** (par, 140, €6): Monasterio Santa María de Sobrado, 628838965, 10am all year, closed 1-4:30pm, in medieval monastery
2. A **Lecer** (28, €10): Casiñas 12b, 981787534, Mar-mid May
3. H **San Marcus** (€40/60): Praza Portal 49, 981787527, mixed reviews

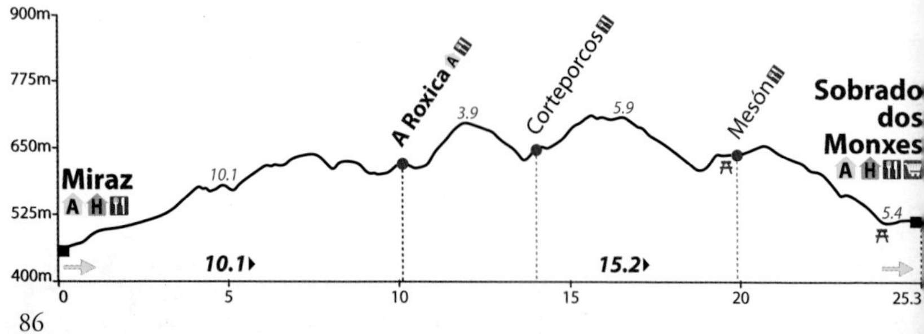

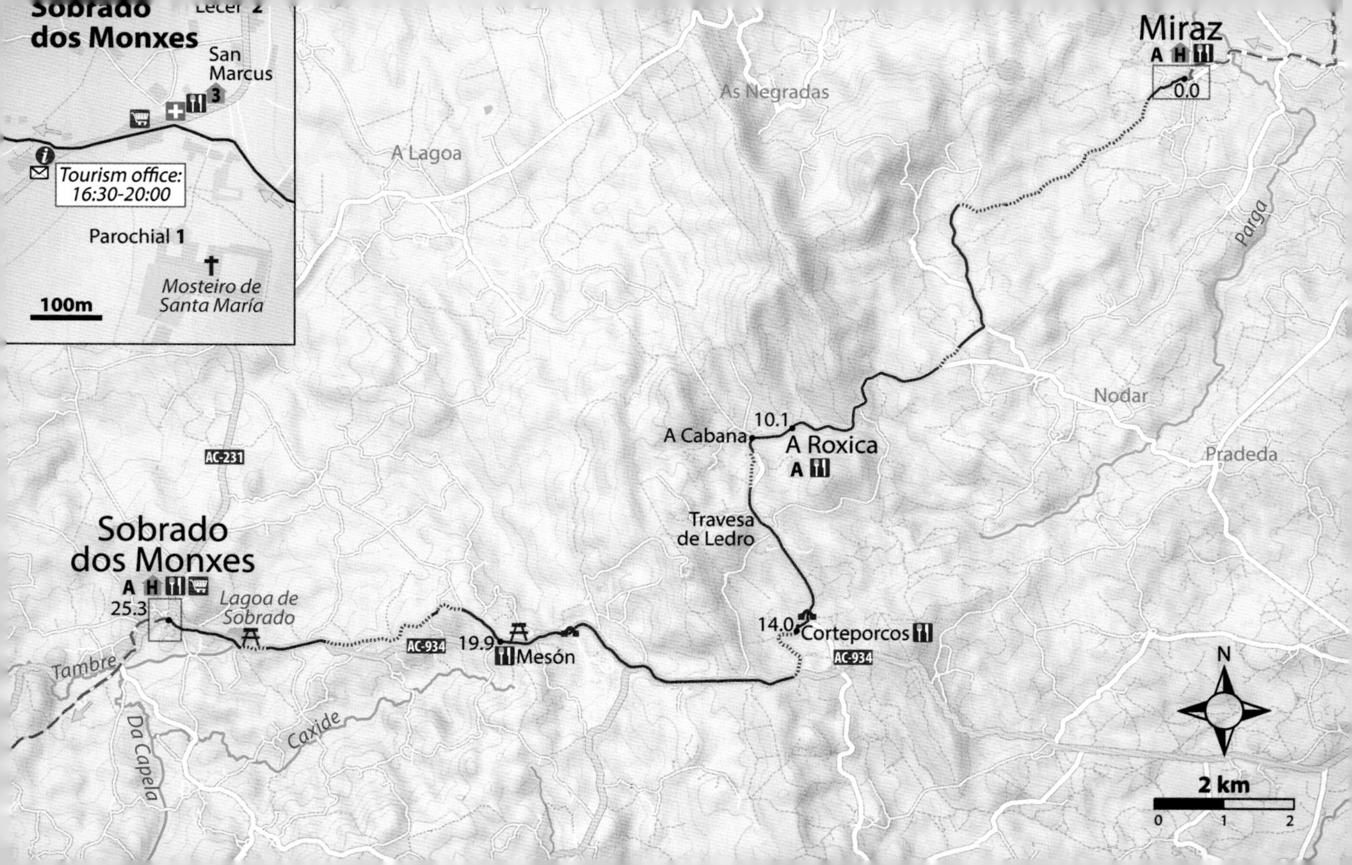
Sobrado dos Monxes
San Marcus
3
Tourism office: 16:30-20:00
Parochial 1
Mosteiro de Santa María
100m
Miraz
A H
0.0
As Negradas
A Lagoa
Parga
Nodar
Pradeda
10.1
A Cabana
A Roxica
A
AC-231
Travesa de Ledro
Sobrado dos Monxes
A H
25.3
Lagoa de Sobrado
19.9
Mesón
AC-934
14.0
Corteporcos
Tambre
Caxide
Da Capela
N
2 km
0
1
2

35

SOBRADO DO MONXES TO ARZUA

21.9km (13.6mi), 6-7.5 HOURS, DIFFICULTY:

P 81%, 17.7km, U 19%, 4.2km

Approaching the Camino Francés, there's one final route decision. On the S end of Boimorto after playground to the L, the ⚠ **route splits:** ❶ L to Arzúa and the Camino Francés for the final 40km to Santiago (recommended, adds 4.3km but much more enjoyable walking). ❷ R, opting for a more direct route and to join the Camino Francés significantly west of Arzúa. On stage 36, this option splits again 9.8km ahead. Stay L to follow an older, more traditional option to join the Camino Francés 6.5km before Arca near Salceda.

12.2 **Boimorto** A H Xunta A is 1.8km before town.

1. A **Xunta** (34, €6): , Cernadela 3, 638392024/981516020, all year
2. A **Gándara** (19, €14/-/48): , Gándara 49, 981516114, a. y.
3. H **Cafe Bar Luis** (€30-35): , Gándara 44, 981516218

21.9 **Arzúa** A H

1. A **Xunta** (48, €6): , Cima de Lugar 6, 660396824, 1pm all year
2. A **De Selmo** (50, €10-12): , Lugo 133, 981939018
3. A **Santiago Apóstol** (72, €10-12): , Lugo 107, 981508132, a. y.
4. A **Don Quijote** (50, €10): , Lugo 130, 981500139, all year
5. A **Ultreia** (39, €10): , Lugo 126, 981500471, all year
6. A **De Camino** (42, €10-12): , Lugo 118, 981500415, Mar-Nov
7. A H **Arzúa** (12, €10/-/30-40): Rosalía Castro 2, 981508233, Feb-Nov
8. A H **Cima do Lugar** (14, €10+/37/47): , Lugar 22, 981500559, a. y.
9. A **The Way** (40, €10-17): , C. Lugar 28, 604051353, Apr-Nov
10. A **Casa del Peregrino** (14, €12): , Cima do Lugar 7, 686708704
11. A H **Pensión del Peregrino** (€15/36/50): , Ramón Franco 7, 981500145
12. A **Caminantes II** (28, €10): , Sant. 14, 647020600, Apr-Oct
13. A H **O Santo** (22, €12/36/-): , 981500957, Apr-Oct
14. A **Da Fonte** (20, €10-12): , Carmen 18, 604002380, Apr-Oct
15. A **Vía Láctea** (60, €10-12): , José N. Vilas 26, 981500581, a. y.
16. H **Hostal Teodora** (€40/50): , Lugo 38, 981500083
17. H **Pensión Rúa** (€35/45): , Lugo 130, 981500139

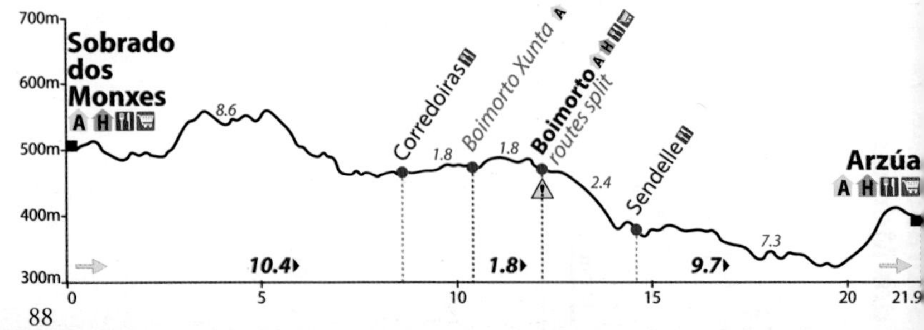

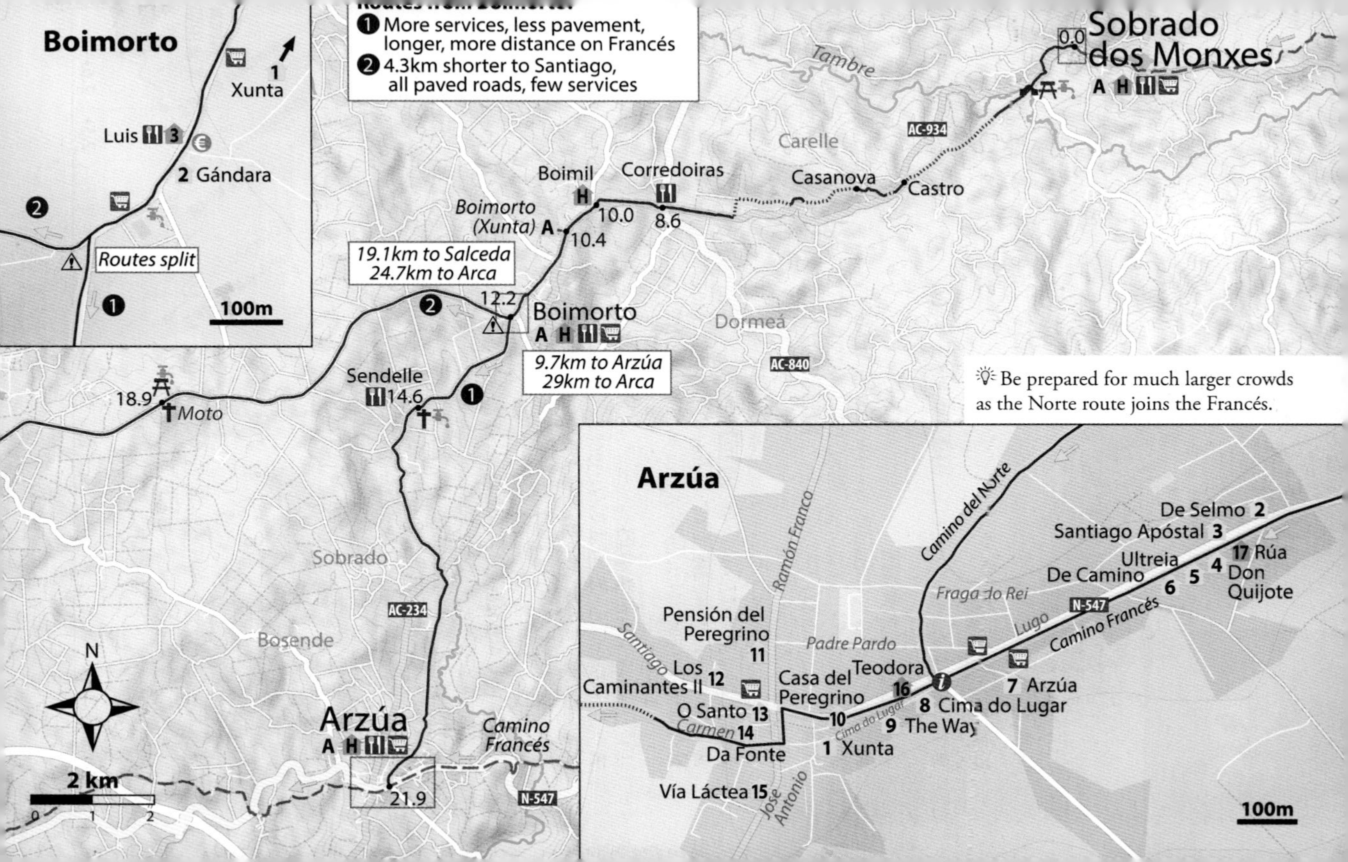
Boimorto
1 Xunta
Luis 3
2 Gándara
Routes split
100m
❶ More services, less pavement, longer, more distance on Francés
❷ 4.3km shorter to Santiago, all paved roads, few services
Sobrado dos Monxes
0.0
A H
Tambre
AC-934
Carelle
Casanova
Castro
Boimil
Corredoiras
8.6
10.0
Boimorto (Xunta) A
10.4
19.1km to Salceda
24.7km to Arca
12.2
Boimorto
A H
9.7km to Arzúa
29km to Arca
Dormeá
AC-840
Be prepared for much larger crowds as the Norte route joins the Francés.
Sendelle
14.6
18.9
Moto
Sobrado
AC-234
Bosende
N
Arzúa
A H
Camino Francés
21.9
N-547
2 km
Arzúa
Camino del Norte
De Selmo 2
Santiago Apóstal 3
Ultreia
De Camino
17 Rúa Don Quijote
4
5
6
Fraga do Rei
N-547
Lugo
Camino Francés
Ramón Franco
Padre Pardo
Pensión del Peregrino 11
Santiago
Los Caminantes II 12
Casa del Peregrino
Teodora
16
7 Arzúa
8 Cima do Lugar
9 The Way
O Santo 13
10
Cima do Lugar
Carmen 14
Da Fonte
1 Xunta
Vía Láctea 15
Jose Antonio
100m

36 ARZUA TO ARCA

19.3km (12.0mi), 5.5-7 Hours, Difficulty:
P 22%, 4.3km, U 78%, 15.0km

Ups and downs through villages from Arzúa. Fragrant eucalyptus groves provide shade.

3.5 Burres A H

A H **Camiño das Ocas** (30, €12/35/45): , 648404780, +400m

8.0 A Calle A

A **Ponte de Ferreiros** (30, €13): , 665641877, all year, +200m

11.4 Salceda A H

A **Boni** (20, €12): , 618965907, Mar-Oct
A H **Alborada** (10, €12/-/50): , 981502956, Apr-Oct
A H **Pousada Salceda** (8, €12/40/47): , N547 km 75, 981502767, +300m

14.2 Brea A H ⚠ El Chalet open Mon-Fri only!

A H **El Chalet** (12, €12/-/40): , A Brea 5, 659380723, Apr-Oct
H **O Mesón** (€32/44): , A Brea 16, 981511040
H **The Way** (€20/34/42): , A Brea 36, 628120202

16.7 Santa Irene A H

A **Xunta** (36, €6): , 660396825, 1pm all year, restaurant +1.5 km
A **Santa Irene** (15, €13): , 981511000, Apr-Oct, charming
A **Astrar** (24, €10-13): , Astrar 18, 608092820, Mar-Nov, +700m

19.3 Arca A H (also O Pino or O Pedrouzo), 638612496,

1. A **Xunta** (120, €6): , Lugo 30, 660396826, 1pm a. y., behind post office
2. A H **O Burgo** (10, €10/28/38): , Lugo 47, 630404138, Apr-Oct
3. A **Porta Santiago** (54, €10): , Lugo 11, 981511103, Mar-Nov
4. A **O Trisquel** (68, €12): , Picón 1, 616644740
5. A **Otero** (36, €10): , Forcarei 2, 671663374, Apr-Oct

Continued on map

600m
500m
400m
300m
200m
Arzúa A H
Burres A H
A Calzada
A Calle A
Salceda A H
routes rejoin
Brea A H
O Empalme
Santa Irene A H
Arca A H
A Rúa
3.5 2.6 1.9 3.4 1.2 1.6 1.2 1.3 1.4 1.2
3.5› 4.5› 3.4› 2.8› 2.5› 2.6›
0 5 10 15 19.3

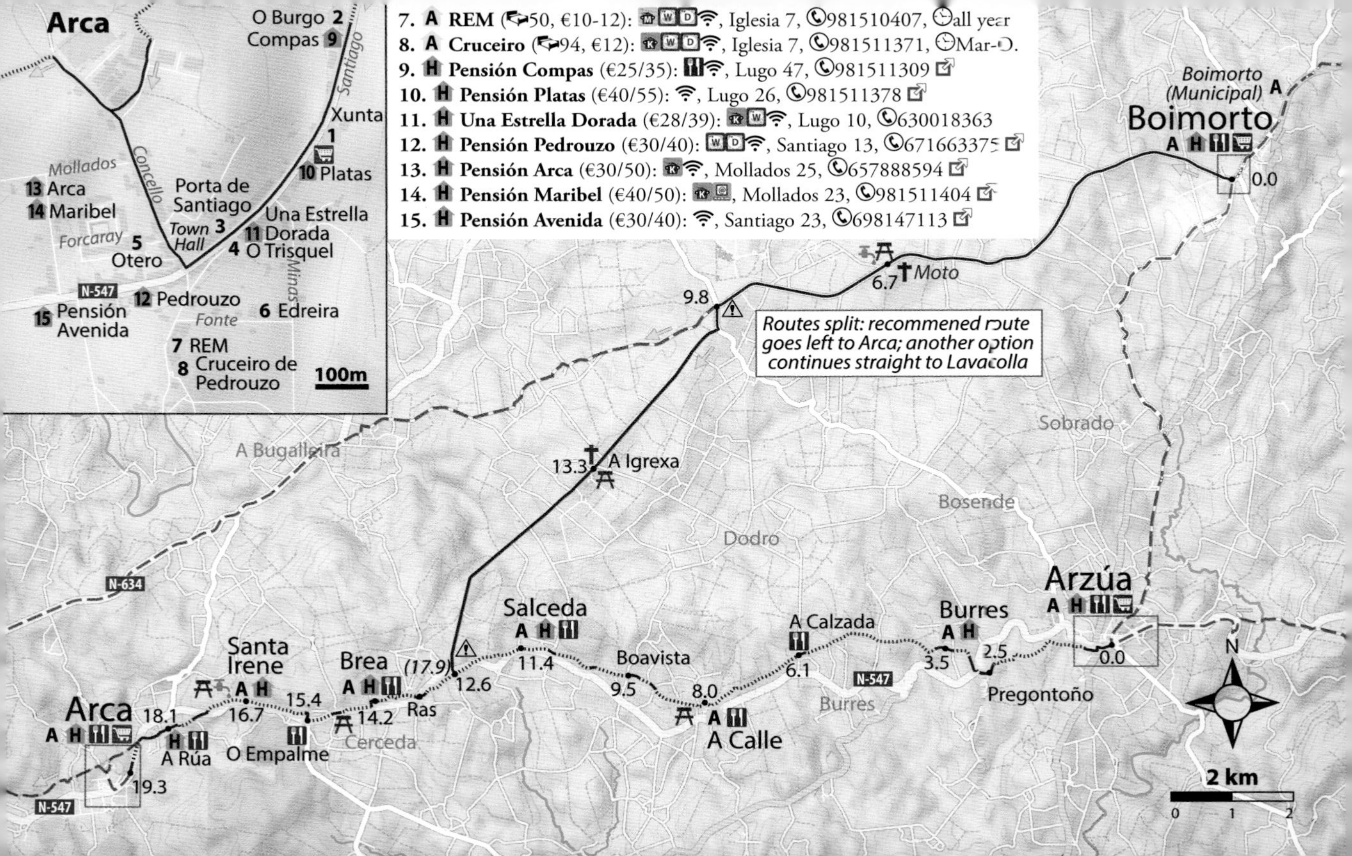
7. A REM (50, €10-12): , Iglesia 7, 981510407, all year
8. A Cruceiro (94, €12): , Iglesia 7, 981511371, Mar-O.
9. H Pensión Compas (€25/35): , Lugo 47, 981511309
10. H Pensión Platas (€40/55): , Lugo 26, 981511378
11. H Una Estrella Dorada (€28/39): , Lugo 10, 630018363
12. H Pensión Pedrouzo (€30/40): , Santiago 13, 671663375
13. H Pensión Arca (€30/50): , Mollados 25, 657888594
14. H Pensión Maribel (€40/50): , Mollados 23, 981511404
15. H Pensión Avenida (€30/40): , Santiago 23, 698147113
Arca
O Burgo 2
Compas 9
Santiago
Xunta
1
10 Platas
Mollados
Concello
13 Arca
14 Maribel
Porta de Santiago
Town Hall 3
Una Estrella
11 Dorada
4 O Trisquel
Forcaray 5
Otero
Minas
N-547
12 Pedrouzo
15 Pensión Avenida
Fonte
6 Edreira
7 REM
8 Cruceiro de Pedrouzo
100m
Boimorto (Municipal) A
Boimorto
A H
0.0
6.7 Moto
9.8
Routes split: recommened route goes left to Arca; another option continues straight to Lavacolla
Sobrado
A Bugalleira
13.3 A Igrexa
Bosende
Dodro
N-634
Arzúa
A H
Salceda
A H
A Calzada
Burres
A H
Santa Irene
A H
Brea
A H
(17.9)
12.6
11.4
Boavista
9.5
8.0
6.1
N-547
3.5
2.5
0.0
N
Pregontoño
Arca
A H
18.1
16.7
15.4
14.2
Ras
Burres
A Calle
A
H
A Rúa
O Empalme
Cerceda
19.3
N-547
2 km
0
1
2

37

ARCA TO SANTIAGO

20.0km (12.4mi), 5.5-7 Hours, Difficulty:
P 83%, 21.2km, U 17%, 4.4km

The path today passes through more eucalyptus forests and several small villages to arrive at Monte do Gozo, within sight (on a clear day) of Santiago's cathedral spires. The last 5km are city walking. The atmosphere entering Santiago is often jubilant, with singing, shouting and congratulations, no matter how dreary the weather. Leave early to arrive in time for the noon pilgrim mass.

3.4 Amenal

H **Hotel Amenal** (€60): W D, Amenal 12, 981510431

10.0 Lavacolla

"place of washing"

A **Lavacolla** (34, €12): W, Lavacolla 35, 981897274
H **A Concho** (€30-35/35-45): , Lavacolla 1, 981888390
H **Casa Lavacolla** (€40-60): , Lavacolla 20, 659881868
H **San Paio** (€38/49): , 981-888205
H **Garcas** (€35/50): , Naval 2, 981888225
H **Ruta Jacobea** (€69): , Lavacolla 41, 981888211
H **Pazo Xan Xordo** (€65): , Xan Xordo 6, 981888259, +900m

14.6 San Marcos

H **Akelarre** (€35-45/40-50): W D, San Marcos 37B, 981552689

15.1 Monte do Gozo

Galician: *Monxoi* "Mount Joy"

A **Xunta** (500, €6): W D, 981558942, 1pm all year, rooms of 8, bunker-like
A **Monte do Gozo (Polskie)** (par, 40, don): W, Rúa das Estelas, 981597222, May-Oct, run by Polish volunteers
H **Santiago Apóstal** (€50-70): W D, San Marcos 1, 981557155

20.0 Santiago de Compostela

See city map and accommodations list on p. 94-95.

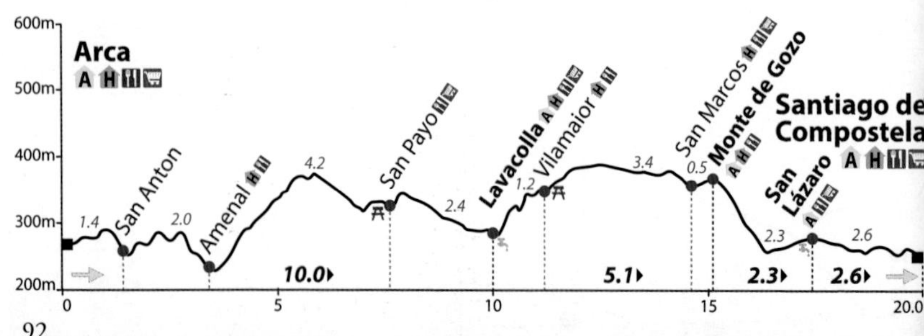

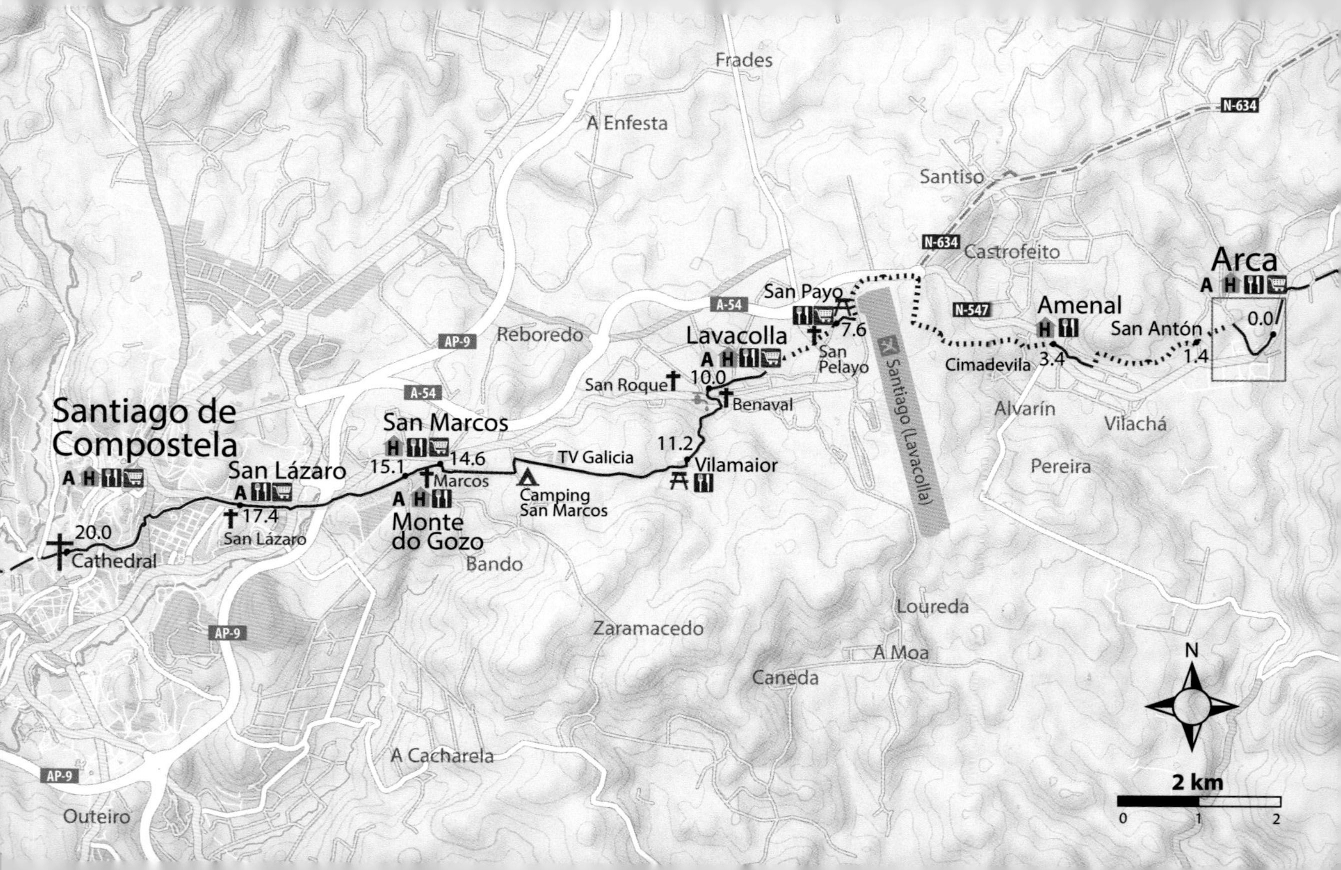

Frades
A Enfesta
Santiso
N-634
N-634
Castrofeito
Arca
A H
0.0
San Antón
1.4
Amenal
H
N-547
Cimadevila
3.4
Alvarín
Vilachá
Pereira
San Payo
A-54
7.6
San Pelayo
Santiago (Lavacolla)
Lavacolla
A H
San Roque
10.0
Benaval
Reboredo
AP-9
A-54
11.2
Vilamaior
TV Galicia
Camping San Marcos
San Marcos
H
14.6
15.1
Marcos
A H
Monte do Gozo
Bando
Santiago de Compostela
A H
San Lázaro
A
17.4
San Lázaro
20.0
Cathedral
AP-9
Loureda
Zaramacedo
A Moa
Caneda
A Cacharela
AP-9
Outeiro
N
2 km
0
1
2

Santiago de Compostela

17.4 San Lazaro/outer Santiago A

1. A **Xunta** (80, €10 first night, €7 for 2nd/3rd): , c/San Lázaro, 981571488, all year
2. A **Fin del Camino** (asoc, 110, €9): Moscova, 981587324, May-Oct
3. A **Santo Santiago** (40, €10-12): , Lázaro Valiño 3, 657402403, all year
4. A **Acuario** (70, €13-20): , Estocolmo 2, 981575438, Mar-Nov
5. A **Monterrey** (36, €12-15): , Fontiñas 65, 655484299, all year
6. A **La Credential** (36, €10-14): , Fonte Concheiros 13, 981068083, Mar-Nov
7. A **La Estrella de Santiago** (24, €10-16): , Concheiros 36-38, 881973926, all year

0 **Santiago de Compostela** A H

Santiago city: Rúa do Vilar 63, 981-555129, Daily 9am-9pm (summer)
Galicia: Rúa do Vilar 30, 902-332010, M-F 10am-8pm, Sa 11am-2pm, 5-7pm, Su 11am-2pm
Pilgrim office: Rúa Carretas 33, 981-568846, Daily M-Sa 9am-9pm (summer), left luggage,
A **Porta Real** (24, €10-20): W D @, Concheiros 10, 633610114, all year
A H **Seminario Menor** (177, €11-15/14-20/28-40): W D @, Quiroga Palacios 2, 881031768, Mar-Oct, all beds not bunks, some reports of theft, lockers available
A **Meiga Backpackers** (hostel, 30, €13-15): W D @, Basquiños 67, 981570846, all year
A **Basquinos 45** (10, €10-16): W D, Basquinos 45, 661894536, all year
A H **La Salle** (20, €17-20/37/59): W D @, Tras Santa Clara, 682158011
A **Fogar de Teodomiro** (hstl, 20, €18): W D @, Algalia de Arriba 3, 981582920, 10am
A H **Linares** (14, €22/60/70): W D, Algalia Abajo 34, 981580443
A H **A Casa Do Peregrino** (€15-20/50-80/60-85): W D, Azabacheria 2, 981573931
A **Last Stamp** (54, €18-25): W D @, Preguntoiro 10, 981563525, mid Jan-mid Dec
A **Azabache** (20, €14-18): W D, Azabachería 15, 981071254, all year
A **Santiago KM-0** (41, €20-25): W D, das Carretas 11, 881974992
A H **Blanco** (20, €12-20/-/35-45): Galeras 30, 881976850
A **Roots and Boots** (hstl., 48, €16-21): W D @, Campo Cruceiro do Galo 7, 699631594
A **Mundoalbergue** (34, €16-18): W D @, San Clemente 26, 981588625, all year
A H **La Estación** (24, €15/30/40): W D, Xoana Nogueira 14, 981594624, all year
A **Compostela** (36, €16-18): W D @, S Pedro de Mezonzo 28, 881017840
H **Altaïr Hotel** (€75/110): Loureiros 12, 981554712
H **Costa Vella** (€60/83): Porta da Pena 17, 981569530, restored Jesuit house
H ☆ **San Martín Pinario** (pilgrim €25/40): Plaza Inmaculada 3, 981560282
H **Dos Reis Católicos** (€160+/180+): Praza do Obradoiro, 981582200, Parador
H **Costa Azul** (€22-40/30-60): Das Galeras 18, 602451906
H **Pensión Fonseca** (40-63/60-70): Fonseca 1, 981584145
H **Hostal Suso** (€58-70): Villar 65, 981586611
H **Pensión Centro** (€30-40/40-50): Senra 11, 981588465

About the Authors

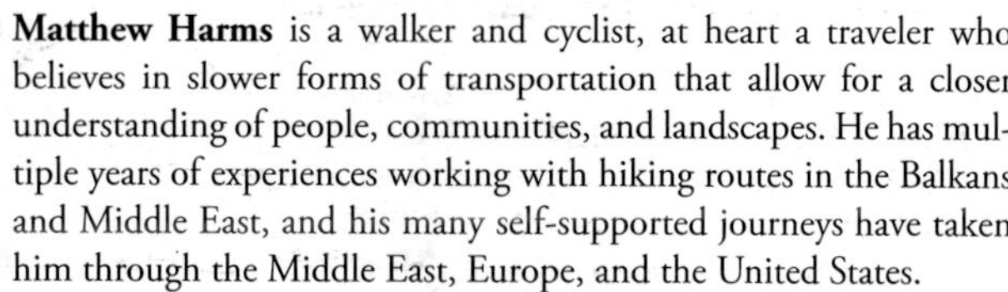

Matthew Harms is a walker and cyclist, at heart a traveler who believes in slower forms of transportation that allow for a closer understanding of people, communities, and landscapes. He has multiple years of experiences working with hiking routes in the Balkans and Middle East, and his many self-supported journeys have taken him through the Middle East, Europe, and the United States.

Anna Dintaman and **David Landis** are the cofounders of Village to Village Press, LLC and bring over 10 years of experience working with walking routes in the Mediterranean and Middle East. Both avid hikers and cyclists, their experience ranges from backpacking Patagonia and Nepal to hiking in the Alps, Andes, and Appalachian mountains to cycling across the United States. They have shared a deep love of the Camino since their first journeys on the Francés route in 2009. In 2007, David cofounded the Jesus Trail, a hiking trail that connects sites from the life of Jesus. They enjoy introducing their children to the joys of walking, the outdoors, and learning from other cultures.

Feedback, comments & corrections welcomed: info@caminoguidebook.com

facebook.com/caminoguidebooks
instagram.com/caminoguidebook
twitter.com/caminoguidebook
pinterest.com/caminoguidebook

Village to Village Press, LLC specializes in publishing hiking guidebooks and supporting trail development projects, especially with an emphasis on pilgrimage along the Camino de Santiago and in the Middle East and Mediterranean regions.